Activities

BASICS FOR A *Biblical* WORLDVIEW

Greenville, South Carolina

Note: The fact that a given writer is cited or quoted in this textbook does not mean that BJU Press endorses that writer from the standpoint of morals, philosophy, or scientific hypotheses. The nature of a worldview book is such that we must cite and quote people with whom we disagree. Part of developing a biblical worldview is cultivating the ability to discern between the good and problematic views of all sorts of people, even Christians.

Basics for a Biblical Worldview, Student Activities

Course Vision and Design
Brian Collins, PhD
Bryan Smith, PhD

Writer
Daniel Olachea, MDiv

Consultant
L. Michelle Rosier

Academic Oversight
Jeff Heath, EdD
Rachel Santopietro, MEd

Editor
Suzanne Villegas, MA

Cover and Book Designer
Michael Asire

Cover Illustrator
Karen Schipper

Illustrators
Patrick Mahoney
Rommel Ruiz

Page Layout
Lydia Thompson

Digital Content Management
Peggy Hargis

Permissions
Tatiana Bento
Carrie Hanna

Project Coordinator
Christopher Daniels

Photo credits appear on page 145.

Acknowledgments appear within the notes, which begin on page 143.

The text for this book is set in Adobe Minion Pro, Adobe Myriad Pro, Avenir, Futura and Futura Condensed by URW, and Oswald by Vernon Adams.

Printed in the United States of America

ISBN 978-1-62856-629-1

15 14 13 12 11 10 9 8 7 6 5 4 3

Worldviews have existed not only in every place but also in every time. People have always wondered about those big questions: Where did I come from? Why am I here? What's wrong with the world? How can things be made right? Where are we all headed in the end? Because every person throughout time has had a worldview, you can observe various worldviews in biblical accounts of ancient history.

Remember that the things people say and do are based on the big story in their head and on their basic beliefs driven by their loves. Since most people don't explain their worldview to others, you can't know their worldview except by what they say and do. As you look at two scenes from biblical history, you will observe what the people say and do and will come to conclusions about their worldviews.

Read the verses and answer the questions.

MEDITERRANEAN SAILORS (790–750 BC)

Jonah 1:1–16

Jonah was on a ship with sailors from other places who had worldviews different from his. Observe their words and actions to find out about their big stories and basic beliefs.

The Joppa coast, where Jonah launched toward Tarshish

1. What did the sailors' reaction to the storm reveal about their big stories? Who did they believe was in control of the world, and what did they think was the status of humans?

___

___

___

2. What did the captain's response to Jonah's sleeping reveal about his basic belief about prayer?

___

___

___

3. What did the sailors do and say that demonstrated their basic beliefs about the cause of storms?

___

___

___

4. What did their questions to Jonah reveal about their big stories? What did they think could cause things to go wrong in the world?

5. What were their basic beliefs about how to respond to the God who had caused the storm?

6. What were their basic beliefs about the value of life?

7. What did their response to the calmed storm reveal about their big stories?

Mars Hill, where Paul preached to the philosophers

ATHENIANS (AD 49)

Acts 17:16–34

Paul was in Athens, the famous Greek city, to preach the gospel. Athenians spent almost all their time studying philosophy. Philosophy is basically an attempt to develop worldviews with human reasoning. It tries to answer those big questions that form a worldview. As a result, many Athenians had well-developed worldviews. Observe their words and actions to find out about their big stories and basic beliefs.

8. What common element in the Athenians' big stories troubled Paul as he looked around the city?

9. What two types of philosophers are mentioned in verse 18?

10. What did some of the philosophers call Paul, indicating the conflict between their basic beliefs and his?

11. What did some of the philosophers say about Paul's preaching, showing that they found his big story to be very different from theirs?

12. Verse 21 reveals something about the philosophers' big stories. No matter what they may have *said* their purpose on earth was, how did their *actions* show what they really believed they were on earth to do?

13. What was their main love, revealed in verse 21?

14. What did Paul first say of them in his message that demonstrated he recognized their worldview based on their actions of idolatry?

15. What did the altar to the unknown god reveal about their big stories?

16. What did their search for new things reveal about their basic beliefs about gods?

17. What did Paul quote from their poets to prove the truth of a big story beginning with God's creation of humans in His image and ending with judgment by Jesus?

18. What does their response to Paul's message indicate about how the idea of a resurrection fit into their big story?

Answer the question based on your answers to the previous questions.

19. How are you able to recognize the worldview of someone else?

____

____

____

BIG STORY ANSWERS

One of the big stories being told today tries to explain how society became broken and how to fix it. The story doesn't include how life started, but it explains the history of society. It interprets the conflicts in history and proposes a solution. The story goes something like this:

> Once upon a time there were many religions, which had a lot of influence in society. These religions had different ideas about right and wrong and about relationships between people and God. These differences caused violent conflicts between religions. The conflicts sometimes affected large numbers of people. But since there is no way to prove scientifically that God exists (so this story goes), it is wrong for people in one religion to persecute those in another religion. The only solution to religious conflicts is for religion to not have influence in public. Religious people can meet with those with similar beliefs as long as they keep their beliefs private. They must not bring those beliefs into the community where people with other faiths also live. The world will find peace when religion stops influencing parts of society like politics and education.

The worldview that tells this story is called secularism. It wants to make society secular—that is, separate from religion. Many people believe this story. They use it to explain the evidence of conflict in the world.

Analyze this big story for its answers to the following big questions of life.

1. Where did society's problems come from?

____

2. Who would be categorized as the "bad guys" in the world?

____

____

3. Who would be categorized as the "good guys"?

____

____

4. What is the only way to prove something?

____

5. What would be the perfect society?

____

____

6. How can that perfect society become a reality?

7. What might be considered the purpose of life?

8. What might be assumed about life after death?

9. What is the best life that someone could hope for?

10. Use some of the questions above to retell a big story that you are familiar with.

LOVE AND BELIEFS

You've learned how love affects the way people see things—themselves, other people, stuff, arguments, stories, and God. What you love affects what you truly believe and how you act on those beliefs.

Read the hypothetical scenarios. Evaluate what you are loving in that situation and what your love is making you believe.

1. You steal answers for a test to improve your grades.

2. You give up the TV so that your little sister can watch a show.

3. You tell someone else about Jesus, even though your friends don't think it's cool.

4. You tithe at your church instead of using everything you earned to buy the latest video game.

5. You stay home to finish an assignment for tomorrow while your friends go shopping.

6. You go to church even though you could be at the big game.

7. You join your friends in smoking even though your parents have told you not to.

____

____

____

8. You make friends with a new student who other students think is weird.

____

____

____

9. You choose to spend your time on social media instead of reading your Bible.

____

____

____

CASE STUDY: FRITZ HABER'S TWO-STORY VIEW

During the career of German scientist Fritz Haber, the world was struggling to produce enough fertilizer to grow the food it needed. The fertilizer that was becoming scarce contained ammonia. Ammonia could be made from the nitrogen in the air, but scientists had not found a way to pull it from the air—until Haber discovered a way. Carl Bosch helped work on the process so that fertilizer could be mass-produced. This process has saved billions of people because of its ability to help grow more crops. It is one of the greatest scientific discoveries of all time. This discovery won Haber the Nobel Prize in Chemistry in 1918.

Not everyone agreed that Haber deserved this award. As a loyal German citizen, Haber had wanted to help his country during World War I. But Germany's actions in the war were against God's law. Haber would have known this through both his Jewish heritage and his Lutheran religion. Yet Haber believed his science was "for humanity in time of peace, for the fatherland [Germany] in time of war." In addition to creating fertilizer, he created explosives and developed a poisonous gas as a weapon. He supervised the first use of his chemical weapon in Belgium to kill Germany's enemies. Haber is now known as the Father of Chemical Warfare.

Haber's life took many tragic turns. His wife committed suicide, possibly because of his work in chemical weapons. His country turned against all Jews, including Haber, during the 1930s. He was exiled from Germany. The rest of Europe condemned his work with chemical weapons. He died in Switzerland with a terrible reputation. His chemicals were eventually used by the Nazis to gas millions of his fellow Jews to death. Haber's own family were some of those killed.

Fritz Haber served the world with science to save billions of lives. His patriotism, however, began to rule his view of right and wrong. He developed terrible weapons that broke international treaties and took the lives of millions.

Answer the questions.

1. How did Fritz Haber help with crop growth?

____

____

____

2. How did Haber help Germany in World War I?

____

____

____

3. How did Haber's work for his country affect his relationship with others?

4. Why did some people dislike that Haber won the Nobel Prize in Chemistry?

5. In what area was Haber doing good work for humanity?

6. Whom did Haber see as his authority during war?

7. Based on your evaluation of Haber's beliefs, how would you describe his two-story view?

8. Based on your evaluation of Haber's actions, how do you think his two-story view came out in each part of his worldview?

MY SENSE OF THE WORLD

You've learned about several things that people use to make sense of their world: a big story, their loves, their authorities, and the way they look at evidence. The following questions will help you draw conclusions from your actions about how *you* make sense of the world. Think carefully and answer honestly based on what you actually think, say, and do—not on what you think should be the "right" answer. See how you make sense of the world.

Answer the questions.

BIG STORY

1. What do you think about when you experience something that you sense is very beautiful?

____

____

2. Whom do you blame for things that go wrong in your life?

____

____

3. Think of a time when someone did something wrong to you. How did you respond?

____

____

4. What gives you hope in your life?

____

____

5. Based on your answers to questions 1–4, how would you describe the big story that you are using to make sense of your world?

____

____

____

____

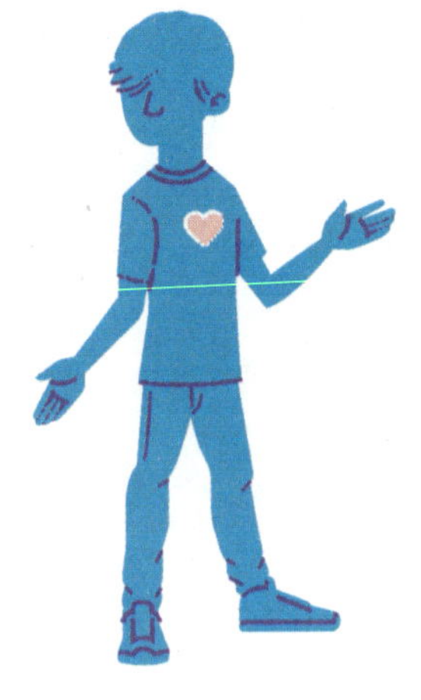

LOVES

6. When you have time that you can use in any way you want, what do you do?

7. What kinds of people do you especially like to be around?

8. When you have money, what do you spend it on?

9. What job would you like to pursue as an adult?

10. Based on your answers to questions 6–9, how would you describe your loves that influence how you make sense of your world?

AUTHORITY

11. When your friends tell you to do something that you know your parents would not approve, whose advice do you actually follow?

12. When you are not sure about a decision, whom do you go to first for advice?

13. Think of a time when you changed your mind about something you believed. Who influenced you enough to change your mind?

14. When you accomplish something, whose approval do you want most for that action?

15. Based on your answers to questions 11–14, how would you describe the influence of your authorities as you make sense of your world?

EVIDENCE

16. You make sense of personal interactions as evidence of how the world truly works. When you see someone do something bad without any consequences, how do you make sense of that?

17. When you go out of your way to do something right but no one notices, how do you make sense of that?

18. When someone talks to you with excitement about God, how do you make sense of that?

19. What personal interactions would you describe as evidence in your sense of friendship?

20. Based on your answers to questions 16–19, what does your interpretation of evidence show about your sense of the world?

____

____

____

____

Evaluate your answers to the previous questions.

21. What are some areas in which what you *say* you believe about the world is inconsistent with how you really *live* in the world?

____

____

____

____

____

____

____

____

OUR BIBLE

Now that you've learned where the Bible came from originally, you might be wondering, *how did we get our Bible in English?*

God used many people to preserve His Word since its initial writing. The Old Testament, written mostly in Hebrew, was preserved by the Jews (Romans 3:1–2). The New Testament, written in Greek, was preserved by local churches as they copied and shared various books with each other. The preservation and spread of the Bible continued through faithful believers who loved the Bible. Over time, the entire Bible has been translated into hundreds of languages, including English. Advancing technology for reading materials helped more and more people access the Bible.

You will follow the process of Scripture preservation in English by researching the following questions. It is a privilege to read God's Word in your own language and to own your own copy. As you research, thank God for His work in many people's lives to accomplish this translation.

Answer the questions with information from your research.

1. In what year was the Wycliffe Bible completed?

   ____

2. What source did John Wycliffe and his followers use for their translation? Why?

   ____

   ____

3. What did Johannes Gutenberg develop to print the first book in Europe? Around what year did he invent this?

   ____

4. How were books copied before Gutenberg's development?

   ____

5. How did Gutenberg's development improve the spread of the Bible?

   ____

   ____

6. During what years did William Tyndale live?

   ____

7. What sources did Tyndale use for his translation, making it more accurate than Wycliffe's, though he was never able to finish?

   ____

8. In what year was Tyndale's New Testament translation published?

   ____

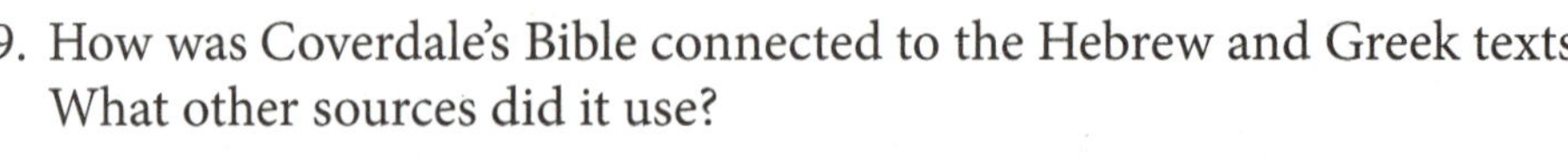

9. How was Coverdale's Bible connected to the Hebrew and Greek texts? What other sources did it use?

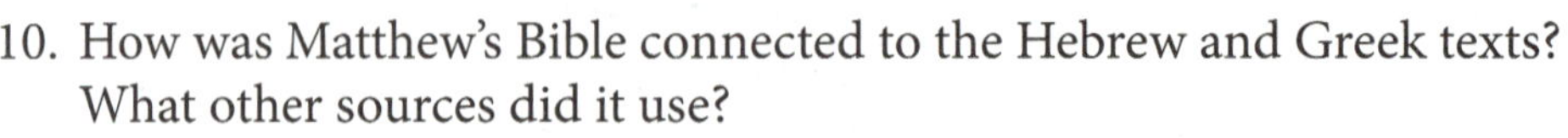

10. How was Matthew's Bible connected to the Hebrew and Greek texts? What other sources did it use?

11. In what year was Matthew's Bible first published?

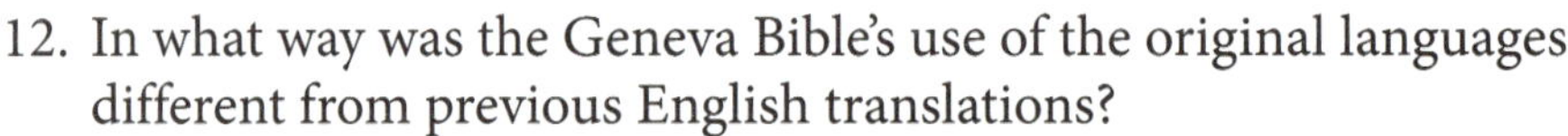

12. In what way was the Geneva Bible's use of the original languages different from previous English translations?

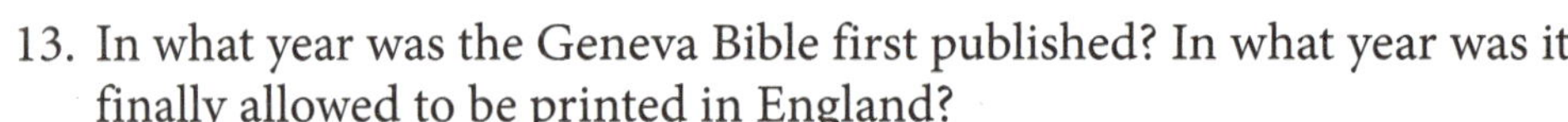

13. In what year was the Geneva Bible first published? In what year was it finally allowed to be printed in England?

14. What original languages was the King James Bible translated from?

15. In what year was the King James Bible first published?

The translation of the English Bible was not without cost. Tyndale and some of his associates were burned at the stake. In response to the work and cost involved for you to have your Bible, write a prayer of thanksgiving for this precious gift from God.

English Bible Timeline: Create a timeline using your answers and add two other events from the 1400s to the present that contributed to the history of the English Bible.

THE MASTER STORYMAKER

When you sit down to read a book, you expect the author to follow some sort of plot structure. If there were no characters, no conflict that needed to be sorted out, and no ending, you probably wouldn't even call it a story. The reason you love a good story—and are able to write your own—is that you're made in the image of the Master Storymaker, God Himself.

God planned the story of the world and revealed much of His planning to us in the Bible. If you look carefully at the Bible, you can see the big picture of God's plan. You will see that He *has* and *will* keep all His promises during the unfolding of the story.

Read the verses and answer the questions.

SETTING THE STAGE

Genesis 1:1

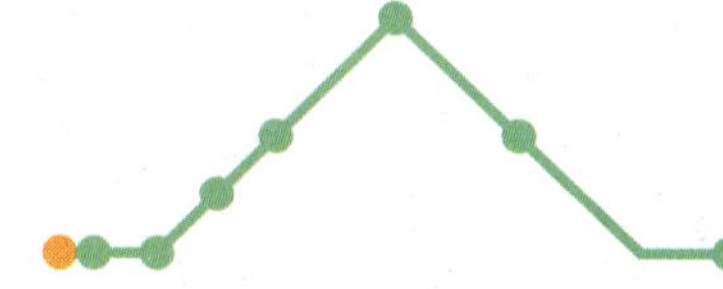

1. What setting did God plan and make for the story of the world?

____

SUMMARY	God would fill this setting with plants and animals. It is the beginning of all that we know.

CHARACTERS

Genesis 1:26–28

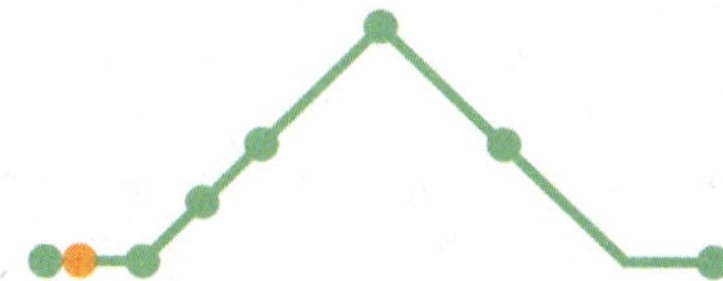

2. Who are the characters God planned in His story?

____

3. What was different about the creation of the characters that indicates they would have a greater role in God's plan than the rest of creation?

____

4. What relationship did God plan for there to be between these characters and the rest of His creation?

____

____

SUMMARY	God created mankind, and He blessed them to both rule and fill the earth. This blessing, along with land and seed (offspring), was the good gift of God to mankind. God wove these themes throughout His story of the world.

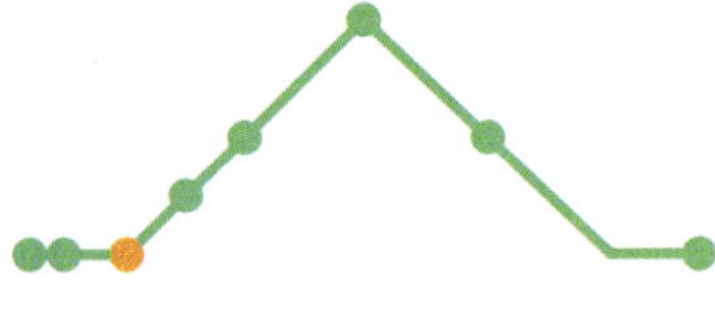

CONFLICT

Genesis 3:14–19

5. What specific conflict is mentioned that came into God's story through mankind's sin? (3:15)

____

____

6. Who did God plan would win the conflict?

____

SUMMARY	Every aspect of what God had given to mankind was affected by sin. Their rule was twisted, the land was cursed, bearing seed would be painful, and the blessed relationship with God was lost.

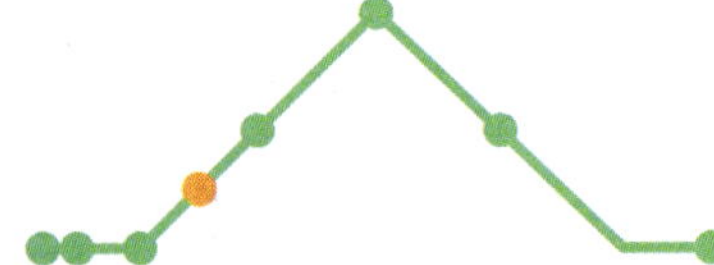

RESOLUTION FORESHADOWING

Isaiah 52:13–53:12

7. What does God say would eventually happen to His Servant? (52:13)

____

8. What will God's righteous Servant do in God's plan? (53:11)

____

SUMMARY	God had a plan in place to restore the blessing of His relationship to many people by placing the penalty of sin on His Servant.

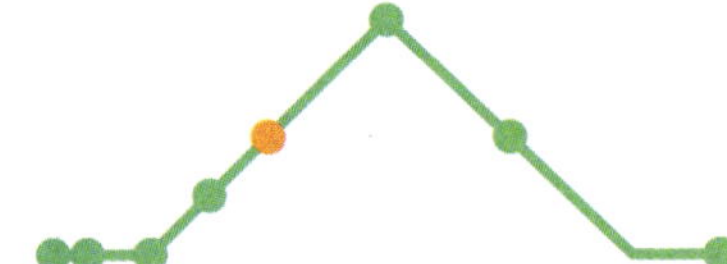

RISING ACTION

Genesis 12:1–3

9. Whom did God include in His plans for blessing?

____

____

Genesis 17:6

10. What did God promise to Abraham to show that He was in control of restoring mankind's fallen rule in His kingdom?

____

Exodus 19:3–6

11. What role that helps people connect with God was Israel to be a kingdom of?

____

2 Samuel 7:8–13, 16

12. What did God promise to David to show that He was in control of restoring mankind's fallen rule in His kingdom?

Jeremiah 31:31, 33–34

13. What did God promise to make with the houses of Israel and Judah?

14. How would the New Covenant restore the relationship between God and those who would become His people?

Ezekiel 36:24–28

15. What would be the results of this work of God in His people?

SUMMARY

God began using a particular family and nation to reestablish His good gifts of land, seed, and blessing and to reestablish mankind's rule in His kingdom.

CLIMAX

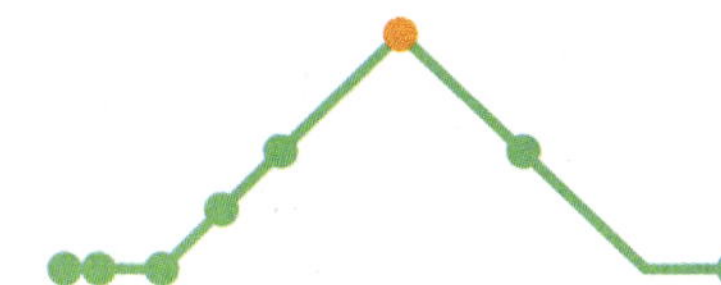

Luke 24:25–27, 44–47

16. Which events did Jesus say were the main fulfillment of all the Old Testament prophecies about the Christ (the Messiah)?

1 Peter 1:18–21

17. Who was known before the world began?

18. How much of this redemption did God plan ahead of time?

SUMMARY

God brought the pieces of His plan together in the person of Jesus Christ in order to redeem the world back to Himself.

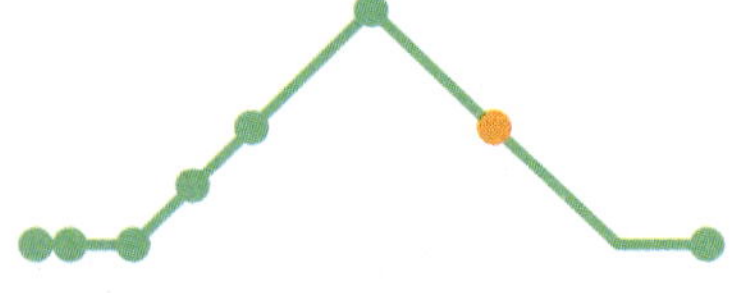

FALLING ACTION

Ephesians 1:4

19. When did God plan for New Testament believers to be part of His story?

Matthew 16:18

20. What did Jesus promise about the church and its enemy, hell?

SUMMARY	God is currently restoring people back to Himself through the church and preparing them to rule well in His world when it is restored to perfection.

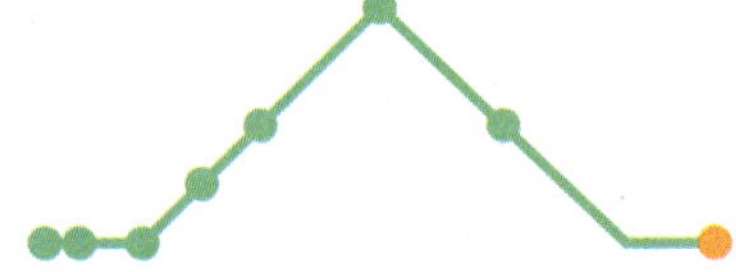

RESOLUTION

Matthew 25:34

21. What will be restored from the original creation?

22. When was the kingdom planned as the end of God's story?

John 17:24

23. What is Jesus' will for His followers at the end of the story?

Revelation 20:11–15

24. What end did God plan for those whose names are not written in the Book of Life?

Revelation 21:1–3

25. What did God plan for the final home of His people?

26. What did God plan for His final relationship with His people?

SUMMARY	God will one day restore the heavens and the earth and restore His people's relationship to Him eternally.

MAKING CONNECTIONS STRUCTURE

God created everything good. Much of that goodness can still be seen and understood in spite of the curse of sin that twists everything. You learned that this original goodness of God's creation is called structure. The Bible can help you understand the structure of many categories.

Read the verses and answer the questions. At the end of each category, use the truths from the verses to summarize the structure God created.

FAMILY

Genesis 2:18–24

1. What is the basic social unit that God created in this account?

2. Why did God give the woman to the man?

3. How is the relationship within this basic social unit described?

Matthew 19:6

4. Because of the relationship between husband and wife, what is their responsibility to each other?

Ephesians 5:22–33

5. What actions are structural in marriage?

6. What does Paul say that the relationship between husband and wife represents?

Genesis 1:28

7. What would be added to the basic social unit when the Creation Mandate was obeyed?

Deuteronomy 6:6–7

8. What responsibility do parents have toward their children?

Exodus 20:12

9. What responsibility do children have toward their parents?

Proverbs 6:20

10. What responsibility do children have toward their parents' teaching?

SUMMARY

SCHOOL

Luke 2:52

11. What did Jesus increase in as a boy?

12. Based on how Jesus grew, what is God's created structure for how children should mature?

Deuteronomy 6:6–7

13. Whom did God command to help children in their instruction?

Proverbs 1:7

14. What did God plan for instruction to start with?

Proverbs 4:10–14

15. How is good instruction "life"?

16. What should a student's response be to verse 13?

2 Timothy 3:15–16

17. What is the source for instruction in righteousness?

18. How should school subjects be based on instruction in righteousness?

SUMMARY

WORK

Genesis 1:28; 2:15

19. What work did God give humans in the beginning? What specific job did God give Adam and Eve?

20. Based on the information from these verses, is work a result of the curse or part of God's created structure?

____

Nehemiah 4:1–6

21. Did the people of Jerusalem have a structural view of work? Explain.

____

____

Colossians 3:23–24

22. What is the result of work?

____

Psalm 90:17

23. To whom does the psalmist look for help with work?

____

Proverbs 24:27

24. Which is the first goal of work, steady income or personal comfort?

____

2 Thessalonians 3:10–12

25. What did Paul command the Thessalonians about work?

____

____

SUMMARY

____

____

____

____

____

____

____

____

Creation, Fall, Redemption Timeline: Place a short description of the created structure of family, school, and work at the Creation point.

MAKING CONNECTIONS FALLENNESS

The Fall has affected every area of life. God created His world to function in a certain way, but the Fall bent that structure away from the way God designed it. Looking around at the world, you can see evidence of fallen direction in everyone's lives in one way or another.

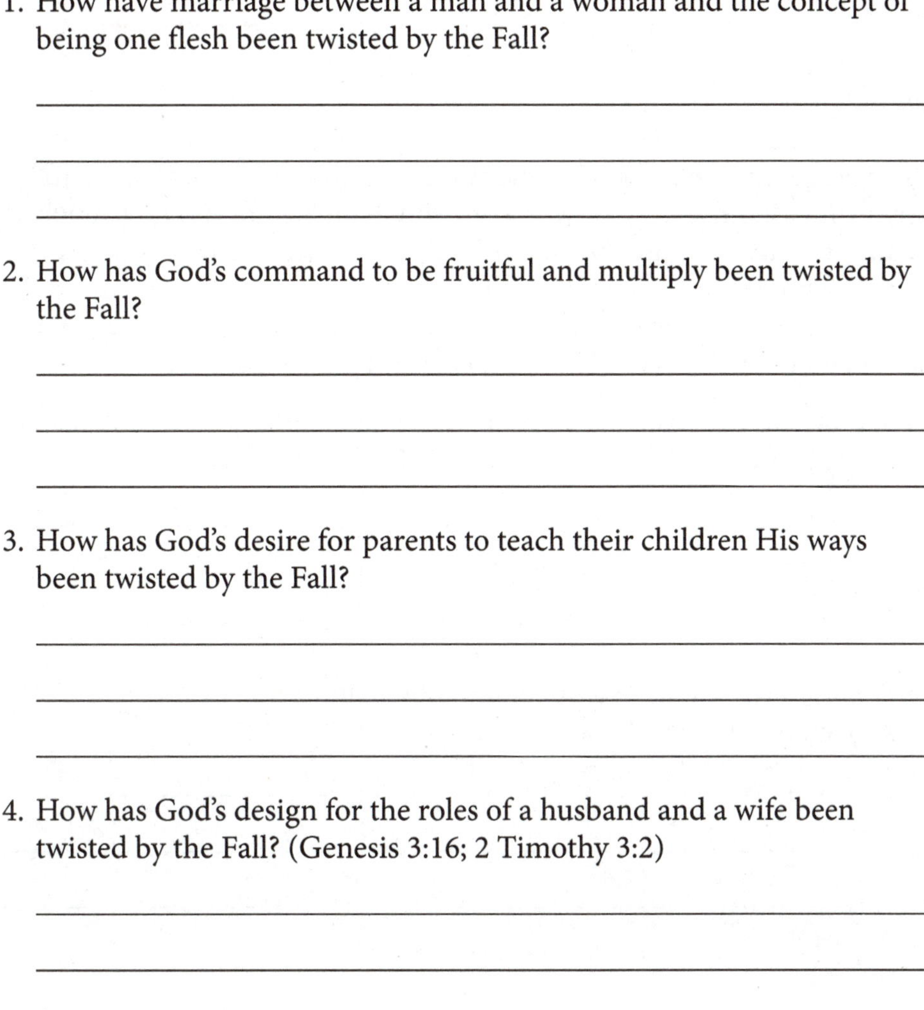

Read the summaries of God's created structure for each category. Answer the questions about how fallen people bend structure in a fallen direction. At the end of each category, summarize the fallen direction.

FAMILY

God created Adam and Eve to be married, to be one flesh as husband and wife. He commands couples to be fruitful and multiply by having children. He wants them to teach their children His ways. God designed a husband's love for his wife to represent God's love for His people, and a wife's submission to her husband to represent the submission of God's people to Him. God desires for children to honor their parents and obey their commands.

1. How have marriage between a man and a woman and the concept of being one flesh been twisted by the Fall?

2. How has God's command to be fruitful and multiply been twisted by the Fall?

3. How has God's desire for parents to teach their children His ways been twisted by the Fall?

4. How has God's design for the roles of a husband and a wife been twisted by the Fall? (Genesis 3:16; 2 Timothy 3:2)

5. How has God's desire for children to honor and obey their parents been twisted by the Fall?

____

____

____

SUMMARY

____

____

____

____

____

____

____

____

SCHOOL

Jesus' example of growing and learning shows that God wants children to be taught in a godly way by godly adults. Like Jesus, children are to increase in wisdom and favor with God and man. School should support that goal, and parents should be helping children in their instruction. Instruction in school should begin with the fear of the Lord. School is important because it helps protect children's lives physically and spiritually. The Bible should guide the purpose and perspective of school instruction.

6. How has the structure of children being taught by godly adults in a godly way been twisted by the Fall? (Judges 2:10–12)

____

____

____

7. How have children's growth in wisdom and favor with God and man been twisted by the Fall?

____

____

____

8. How has the truth that wisdom and instruction begin with the fear of the Lord been twisted by the Fall?

9. Proverbs 4:13 says that good instruction is life. How have people's responses to good instruction been twisted by the Fall?

SUMMARY

WORK

God created work to be good. God commands humans to work at subduing the earth and having dominion over it. Knowing God's purpose for work allows people to work with a good attitude. Work brings rewards, but it is also dependent on God's help. Work is the primary means of providing income and a secondary means of providing comfort. God says that work is required in order to eat.

10. How has people's understanding of work as a created structure been twisted by the Fall?

11. How has working with the right attitude been twisted by the Fall?

12. How has dependency on God for help in work been twisted by the Fall?

13. How has working for income to provide one's needs before personal comfort been twisted by the Fall?

14. How has the requirement of work for eating been twisted by the Fall?

SUMMARY

Creation, Fall, Redemption Timeline: Place a description of fallen direction at the point of the Fall.

SEEING CHRIST IN THE BIBLE'S STORY

In Section 2.5 you learned several titles given to the Hero of God's story because of the roles He played. You will see how these roles are developed with more and more information throughout the Bible.

Read the verses and answer the questions.

SEED OF THE WOMAN

Genesis 3:14–15

1. In the curse on the serpent, what did God promise about the Seed of the woman and the serpent?

Genesis 8:20–22

2. What did God promise to Noah that He would not do again?

3. What would continue while the earth remains?

4. How will the promised stability of the world help the coming of the Seed of the woman?

Genesis 12:1–3

5. What clause shows that God was promising to Abraham (Abram) a seed, or offspring?

6. What did God promise about all families of the earth?

7. How could the original promise about the Seed of the woman possibly connect with God's promise to bless all families of the earth through Abraham?

____

____

____

8. Based on these promises, the Seed of the woman would also be the seed of whom?

____

2 Samuel 7:12–16

9. What did God promise to David about his seed?

____

____

10. How could the original promise about the Seed of the woman possibly connect with God's promise to give David an eternal King on his throne? (1 Corinthians 15:24–25)

____

____

11. Based on these promises, the Seed of the woman would also be the seed of whom?

____

12. God promised a Seed to Abraham and David as fathers, but He also promised a Seed to a woman, a virgin. When was a child born to a woman without a husband to fulfill this promise?

____

REDEEMER

Romans 5:6–8

13. In whose place did Christ die?

____

14. What did Christ's death prove, or demonstrate?

____

Galatians 3:7–14, 16

15. How did Christ make redemption from the curse of the law possible?

____

16. What promise does Christ's death make possible?

17. How do people receive this promise?

18. How do verses 14 and 16 show that God's promises to Abraham were fulfilled?

2 Corinthians 5:18–21

19. What did God do for us by Jesus Christ?

20. What did God make Christ on our behalf?

21. How was Christ righteous?

22. What are we made when we are "in" Christ?

SECOND ADAM

1 Corinthians 15:45–49

23. What did the Second (last) Adam become?

24. Where was the Second Adam from?

25. Based on your answers above, who is the Second Adam?

26. Whose image will believers bear, just as they bore the image of Adam?

THE CHURCH'S HOPE IN TRIALS

What do you do when you face hard times? If you are a believer, it is important for you to consider your role in God's plan of redemption to help you face trials and temptations. Believers throughout history have found that God in His wisdom places them in difficult circumstances where they can use their hope to point others to Him.

Read the verses and answer the questions. At the end, summarize the church's role in God's plan of redemption while they are suffering.

1 Peter 1:3–9

1. How has God given believers a living hope?

2. What keeps believers until the revelation of full salvation?

3. What can bring heaviness, or grief, to believers?

4. What is the result of the testing of believers' faith?

5. Based on these verses, how can believers have hope in trials?

1 Peter 2:11–15

6. What does Peter urge believers to avoid?

7. What will result from their good response to unbelievers' accusations?

8. For whose sake do believers obey those in authority?

9. What effect will believers' good works have on foolish men?

1 Peter 2:18–23

10. Who is the believer's example of suffering for doing right?

11. How did Christ endure when He was treated so badly though He was innocent?

1 Peter 3:14–17

12. Instead of being afraid of what people might say, what should every believer be ready with?

13. What causes unbelievers to be ashamed after they accuse believers?

14. What does Peter say about suffering for doing wrong? Why?

15. Whom is God using to spread His message of hope?

SUMMARY

Creation, Fall, Redemption Timeline: Place the church age (beginning with Pentecost up to the present) on your timeline. Place yourself on the timeline with a description of the believer's redemptive responsibilities during suffering from your summary above.

GOD'S PLAN OF RESTORATION

In Section 2.6 you learned that God has a plan to redeem His people from the physical results of the Fall. The following verses speak of God's full redemption which will restore all things through Christ's resurrection.

Read the verses and answer the questions.

1 Corinthians 15:20–26, 42–49

1. How is Christ's resurrection the first taste of full redemption?

2. When will this full redemption of believers happen?

3. How will Christ restore God's full, righteous dominion over the earth?

4. What is the last enemy of full redemption?

5. How do verses 42–43 describe the fallen, natural body?

6. How are these three problems contrasted in the new redeemed body?

7. Whose image will believers' bodies bear?

Creation, Fall, Redemption Timeline: Full restoration will take place only when Christ returns. Place the second coming of Christ at an unknown point in the near future. Include a description of Christ's restoration of believers and the rest of creation (Romans 8:18–23; Revelation 21:1–4).

Analyze this chart, which describes the Creation, Fall, and Redemption of three categories: the image of God, the Creation Mandate, and mankind's relationship with God. Read the verses and complete the chart with redemptive direction.

Image of God	
Creational Structure	**Genesis 1:27** Mankind was made like God.
Fallen Direction	**Genesis 4:8** Mankind became sinful, selfish, and rebellious against God.
Redemptive Direction	**Romans 8:29; 1 John 2:2**
Creation Mandate	
Creational Structure	**Genesis 1:28** Mankind was given dominion over the earth.
Fallen Direction	**Genesis 4:16–17** Mankind attempted dominion selfishly and independently of God.
Redemptive Direction	**Revelation 11:15; 22:3–5**
Relationship with God	
Creational Structure	**Genesis 3:8** Mankind had a perfect relationship with God.
Fallen Direction	**Isaiah 59:2** Mankind was separated from God by sin.
Redemptive Direction	**2 Corinthians 5:17–19**

"FOLLOW YOUR HEART"

Popular people say a lot of things that their fans quote as great wisdom. How can you tell what's really wise or not? Figuring out which ideas are right or wrong is what discernment is all about. You have to discern what is God's structure for creation and where people have bent that in a fallen direction. Here are some of those quotations for you to check against the Bible for fallen direction.

Read the quotations and use the verses to answer the questions with biblical discernment.

> TRUST YOUR OWN INSTINCTS, GO INSIDE, FOLLOW YOUR HEART. RIGHT FROM THE START, GO AHEAD AND STAND UP FOR WHAT YOU BELIEVE IN. AS I'VE LEARNED, THAT'S THE PATH TO HAPPINESS.
>
> —LESLEY ANN WARREN, AMERICAN ACTRESS

Jeremiah 17:9

1. If your beliefs are based on your own heart, will they be based on truth? Explain.

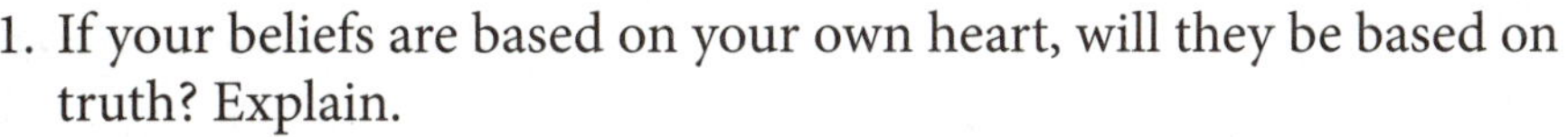

____

____

Proverbs 28:26

2. Proverbs uses just one word to describe the inner being of a person, including both the heart and mind. According to this verse, why should you not trust your heart-mind?

____

____

> I ALWAYS BELIEVED THAT WHEN YOU FOLLOW YOUR HEART OR YOUR GUT, WHEN YOU REALLY FOLLOW THE THINGS THAT FEEL GREAT TO YOU, YOU CAN NEVER LOSE, BECAUSE SETTLING IS THE WORST FEELING IN THE WORLD.
>
> —RIHANNA, BARBADIAN SINGER-SONGWRITER

Ecclesiastes 9:3

3. What is the problem with following "things that feel great to you"?

____

____

Proverbs 14:12

4. Why is it not true that if you follow your heart you cannot lose?

YOUR HEART AND YOUR INSTINCTS ARE FAR MORE RELIABLE THAN YOUR BRAIN. WHEN YOU FOLLOW YOUR HEART, YOU CAN BE SURE YOU WON'T REGRET IT LATER. EVEN IF YOU CALCULATE YOUR EVERY MOVE, IT'S NOT LIKE LIFE EVER GOES ACCORDING TO PLAN.

—NITHYA MENEN, INDIAN ACTRESS

Proverbs 12:8

5. Here again, Proverbs uses one word for the heart-mind. According to this verse, what is the real difference between the ways a person could use his heart-mind?

James 1:14–15

6. Why is it not true that you won't regret following your heart?

I'M HERE TO SPREAD A MESSAGE OF HOPE. FOLLOW YOUR HEART. DON'T FOLLOW WHAT YOU'VE BEEN TOLD YOU'RE SUPPOSED TO DO.

—J. COLE, AMERICAN RAPPER

Proverbs 12:15

7. Why should you not follow your heart but instead follow the things you've been told?

Proverbs 19:21

8. What will actually stand, or be accomplished?

MAKE SURE THAT YOU ALWAYS FOLLOW YOUR HEART AND YOUR GUT, AND LET YOURSELF BE WHO YOU WANT TO BE, AND WHO YOU KNOW YOU ARE. AND DON'T LET ANYONE STEAL YOUR JOY.

—JONATHAN GROFF, AMERICAN ACTOR

Matthew 15:18–19

9. How is it a problem to "be who you want to be"?

____

____

Habakkuk 3:17–18

10. What does Jonathan Groff imply is the source of your joy?

____

11. What do these verses say should be the source of your joy?

____

FAITH THAT IT'S NOT ALWAYS IN YOUR HANDS OR THINGS DON'T ALWAYS GO THE WAY YOU PLANNED, BUT YOU HAVE TO HAVE FAITH THAT THERE IS A PLAN FOR YOU, AND YOU MUST FOLLOW YOUR HEART AND BELIEVE IN YOURSELF NO MATTER WHAT.

—MARTINA MCBRIDE, AMERICAN SINGER-SONGWRITER

12. What word makes this quotation sound like biblical advice?

____

13. How do you know that Martina McBride was not using that word biblically?

____

____

14. Which part of a worldview is obvious from all these quotations?

____

Read the verses and answer the questions. Summarize what the Bible says is the right alternative to following your heart.

Proverbs 3:5–6

15. How can these verses give you more confidence than the advice from the quotations?

____

____

Psalm 119:10–11

16. What can you do to keep your heart from leading you astray?

____

____

SUMMARY

____

____

____

____

MAKING CONNECTIONS REDEMPTION

You have looked at both the structure and the fallen direction in family, school, and work. Now you are ready to complete this Making Connections chart with actions that people can take to push each category in a redemptive direction.

Read the verses and complete the chart.

Family	
Creational Structure	God created Adam and Eve to be married, to be one flesh as husband and wife. He commands couples to be fruitful and multiply by having children. He wants them to teach their children His ways. God designed a husband's love for his wife to represent God's love for His people, and a wife's submission to her husband to represent the submission of God's people to Him. God desires for children to honor their parents and obey their commands.
Fallen Direction	Many people disregard God's design for marriage between a man and a woman. Couples live together and refuse to get married, or they divorce once married. People refuse to have children. People fail to teach their children about God or even abuse them. Husbands refuse to love their families and rule them well. Wives refuse to submit to their husbands. Children refuse to honor and obey their parents.
Redemptive Direction	**Matthew 19:4–6** **Ephesians 5:22–33** **Deuteronomy 6:6–7** **Exodus 20:12** **Proverbs 6:20**

School	
Creational Structure	Jesus' example of growing and learning shows that God wants children to be taught in a godly way by godly adults. Like Jesus, children are to increase in wisdom and favor with God and man. School should support that goal, and parents should be helping children in their instruction. Instruction in school should begin with the fear of the Lord. School is important because it helps protect children's lives physically and spiritually. The Bible should guide the purpose and perspective of school instruction.
Fallen Direction	Many teachers and parents are not godly and do not teach in a godly way. Teachers and parents teach children that there is no God or that they do not need to know Him. Teachers and parents attempt to teach without God's wisdom or the Bible. Students refuse to seek instruction and even rebel against it.

Redemptive Direction	**Luke 2:52** **Deuteronomy 6:6–7** **Proverbs 1:7** **Proverbs 4:13** **2 Timothy 3:15–16**
Work	
Creational Structure	God created work to be good. God commands humans to work at subduing the earth and having dominion over it. Knowing God's purpose for work allows people to work with a good attitude. Work brings rewards, but it is also dependent on God's help. Work is the primary means of providing income and a secondary means of providing comfort. God says that work is required in order to eat.
Fallen Direction	Many people do not think work is a good gift from God. Workers do their jobs with a bad attitude. They do not depend on God to do good work. People try to get as much personal comfort as possible without earning what they need to get it. People want their needs to be provided for without having to work.
Redemptive Direction	**Genesis 1:28** **Nehemiah 4:6** **Colossians 3:23–24** **Proverbs 24:27** **2 Thessalonians 3:10**

Read the verses and answer the questions.

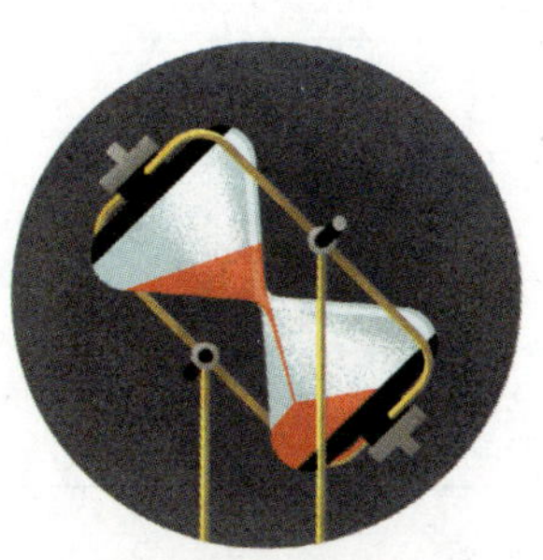

ETERNAL

Psalm 90:2

1. How does this verse demonstrate that God is eternal?

____

____

UNCHANGING

Malachi 3:5–6

2. How do God's people see His unchanging nature in action?

____

____

ALL-POWERFUL (OMNIPOTENT)

Revelation 1:8

3. How does this verse demonstrate that God is omnipotent?

____

____

Luke 1:37

4. Why do you need to know this truth from God about His promises?

____

____

PRESENT EVERYWHERE (OMNIPRESENT)

Acts 17:27–28

5. How does this verse demonstrate that God is omnipresent?

____

____

Psalm 139:7–10

6. What question did the psalmist use to show that God is omnipresent?

____

____

7. What extremes did the psalmist use to show God's omnipresence?

ALL-KNOWING (OMNISCIENT)

Psalm 139:4

8. How does this verse demonstrate that God is omniscient?

1 Samuel 16:7

9. How did God explain to Samuel that He is omniscient?

THE TRINITY

Matthew 28:19

10. What singular and plural contrast in this verse demonstrates the *triunity* of God?

John 1:1–3

11. How do these verses show the Word to be God, one of the persons of the Trinity?

Acts 5:3–4

12. How do these verses show the Holy Spirit to be God, one of the persons of the Trinity?

TRUTH ACCORDING TO GOD

What is truth? Philosophy has always tried to answer this question. Too often, however, unbelieving philosophers seek truth while denying God and His place as Creator and sustainer of the world. Since the fear of the Lord is the beginning of wisdom, these philosophers cannot actually begin to define *truth*. Section 3.2 explained that truth is *reality as interpreted by God*. Because God is the source of truth, you will learn about God Himself as you learn about truth. You will identify the connections the Bible makes between truth and God's own nature and actions.

Read the verses and complete the chart.

	What I Learn about Truth	What I Learn about God
John 17:15–17		God is the source of truth.
Psalm 119:89		God's Word is eternal.
Titus 1:2	Truth is the only thing God speaks, which includes His promises for the future.	
John 17:3	I can know truth.	
John 14:6		
John 1:14	The fullest display of truth in a human is Jesus.	
John 14:16–17	Truth continues to be known through the Holy Spirit after Jesus' ascension. The world rejects truth.	
1 John 5:6		The Holy Spirit's job is to bear witness, or testify, about Jesus.

Use the completed chart to summarize two things: a definition of *truth* and the connections between truth and God's nature and actions.

SUMMARY

SUMMARY

You should recognize from Section 3.3 that God has built into each person a sense of what is good and what is evil. You should also understand that because of our fallen nature, we still need God to give us a true standard of what is good. This is the standard of good from above.

Read the verses and answer the questions. At the end of each category, use the truths from the verses to summarize a definition.

GOOD

Psalm 100:5

1. Who is the ultimate standard of good?

____

2. How is this goodness demonstrated toward humans?

____

____

Nehemiah 9:13

3. What is described as good?

____

4. How do the truths from this verse and Psalm 100:5 connect to each other?

____

____

Matthew 22:37–39

5. How do the truths from these verses and Nehemiah 9:13 connect to each other?

____

____

Luke 10:38–42

6. What did Jesus affirm was good?

____

7. What did Jesus imply was not good?

____

8. How do the truths from these verses and Matthew 22:37–39 connect to each other?

____

____

Psalm 73:28

9. What is described as good?

____

10. How did Mary follow the truth of this psalm in Luke 10:38–42?

____

____

Romans 7:7–12

11. What was God's good law designed to bring?

____

12. Why did the law fail to bring this?

____

13. What did the law teach Paul?

____

Lamentations 3:26

14. What is described as good?

____

____

15. How does this verse give the solution to the problem in Romans 7:7–12?

____

SUMMARY

____

____

____

____

EVIL

James 1:13

16. In what ways is God separate from evil?

Mark 7:20–23

17. Where does evil dwell?

18. How do evil actions come from the heart?

19. What things did Jesus say are evil?

1 Timothy 6:10

20. How is the love of money the root of all kinds of evil?

Hebrews 3:12

21. What is evidence of an evil heart?

SUMMARY

In Section 3.4 you learned that God Himself is beautiful (Psalm 27:4). God's beauty includes His moral perfection. In other words, His moral perfection is the ultimate expression of beauty.

Not only is God beautiful, but He also created beautiful things. All that is beautiful received its beauty from Him. Though the Bible talks about beauty, it doesn't give us a complete definition. We discern what is beautiful according to the order of creation around us and according to God's moral perfection.

Based on the work of many non-Christian and Christian writers over many centuries, Bible teacher R. C. Sproul describes how to discern created order in the arts. He gives four basic principles.

1 PROPORTION

A composition with proportion presents objects or parts of an object as how they truly are in relation to each other. If you've ever tried to draw people, you know that proportion can be difficult to get right. Music and writing must balance tension with resolution.

2 HARMONY

Certain musical tones fit well together. Certain colors work well together. Poets use literary devices to create harmony in a line or stanza. A composition has harmony when all the pieces work together to make the whole better.

3 SIMPLICITY

A carefully written melody need not be complicated to be beautiful all by itself. A simple line in a painting can elegantly depict the form of something. The best stories include simple language to help the reader understand the meaning.

4 COMPLEXITY

Together, simple melodies played on different instruments can create a great musical composition. Paintings with multiple colors and layers create interest and depth. Complexity means that simple parts have been purposefully brought together.

These principles have been masterfully created by God and are His gifts to mankind. Since God made us in His image, we have the ability to appreciate beauty—whether or not we know all the details or terms for describing it.

We're all pleased by a well-written story, meticulously crafted art, the flawless performance of a master musician, or even tasteful furniture arranged by an interior designer. All these things show the handiwork of the artist and are considered beautiful.

Does this mean that everything humans make is beautiful? Or can God's gifts of order be corrupted? Certainly, something evil can be twisted to seem beautiful (Genesis 3:1–6). But only when art, music, design, and literature reflect the order and moral perfections of God can they be truly beautiful.

What about physical beauty? The Bible acknowledges the beauty of human beings. Some may be remarkably pleasing, but every person has a unique beauty (Psalm 139:14) because each one is made in God's image. A Christian also has inner beauty—spiritual qualities that reflect God's character. This beauty increases the more Christians seek God's will and purposes for their lives.

Answer the questions.

1. Where does beauty originate? (Psalm 27:4; Genesis 2:9)

____

2. Why are we able to appreciate beauty? (Genesis 1:26–27)

____

3. How can we make things that are beautiful?

____

____

4. What are four principles of beauty?

____

____

5. How do these four principles of beauty relate to God's creation?

____

____

6. How does a Christian become more beautiful?

____

____

EVALUATING BEAUTY

Remember these four principles of beauty introduced in the previous activity? You will practice evaluating paintings and musical compositions for beauty with these principles.

Proportion: All parts balanced in relationship to the whole and each other
Harmony: Various parts working together to enhance the whole
Simplicity: Clean, minimalistic design that is understandable
Complexity: Many purposeful details creating interest and depth

Examine and evaluate the following paintings using the four principles.

The Night Watch
by Rembrandt van Rijn

1. What elements of this painting contribute to its beauty?

The Great Wave off Kanagawa
by Katsushika Hokusai

2. What elements of this painting contribute to its beauty?

The Hay Wain
by John Constable

3. What elements of this painting contribute to its beauty?

Composition VII
by Wassily Kandinsky

4. What element seems most distorted in this painting?

____

____

____

____

Daniel-Henry Kahnweiler
by Pablo Picasso

5. What element seems most distorted in this painting?

____

____

____

____

Reflection of the Big Dipper
by Jackson Pollock

6. What element seems most distorted in this painting?

____

____

____

____

Listen to and evaluate the following musical compositions using the four principles.

"Canon in D Major"
by Johann Pachelbel

7. What elements of this composition contribute to its beauty?

Rondo from Horn Concerto No. 4 in E-flat
by Wolfgang Amadeus Mozart

8. What elements of this composition contribute to its beauty?

Finale of *Firebird Suite*
by Igor Stravinsky

9. What elements of this composition contribute to its beauty?

"Wana Baraka"
(Kenyan folk song)

10. What elements of this composition contribute to its beauty?

Allegro from Violin Concerto
by Alban Berg

11. What element seems most distorted in this composition?

Music for Piano
by John Cage

12. What element seems most distorted in this composition?

____

____

____

LOVE ACCORDING TO GOD

Section 3.5 helped you understand love based on who God is and what He has done. Now you also understand what His love should mean to you. Look up these verses in your own Bible or reread the portions of Section 3.5 that mention these verses as you review these concepts.

Read the verses and answer the questions.

John 3:16

1. What does this famous verse say about love?

John 15:13

2. How did Jesus demonstrate His great love for us?

Matthew 22:35–40

3. How does love for God and neighbor relate to the law?

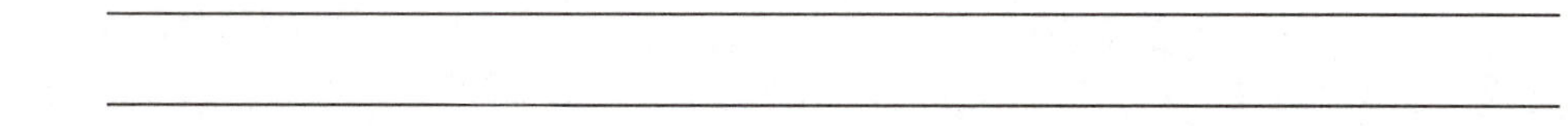

1 Corinthians 13:3

4. Does this verse prove that love can be completely defined as self-sacrificial giving? Explain.

Luke 11:42–43

5. How did the Pharisees’ actions support the idea that love is “your heart going out to something”?

1 John 4:8

6. Who is the standard for love?

____

7. What does this verse reveal about those who do not love?

____

1 John 4:19

8. Who first loved?

____

9. What should be our response to this love, according to the verse?

____

John 17:24

10. How does this verse prove that love is eternal?

____

____

Romans 8:38–39

11. What can separate us from the love of God?

____

Identify each way of showing love from the verses.

Ways to Show Love	
John 3:16	
John 15:13	
Psalm 103:13	
John 14:15	
Ruth 1:16	

GOD, FOR HIS GLORY . . .

Read the verses and find what works of God they are describing. Write a sentence of what God did or does for the reason given on each chart. At the end, summarize your findings into a paragraph explaining the reason for God's works.

For His Sake	
2 Kings 19:31–34	
Isaiah 43:22, 25	
Isaiah 48:10–11	
Matthew 10:39	
2 Corinthians 12:9–10	
Philippians 1:29	

For His Name's Sake	
1 Samuel 12:22	
Psalm 23:3	
Psalm 106:7–8	
Isaiah 48:9	
Ezekiel 20:9	
1 John 2:12	

For His Praise	
Psalm 40:3	
Isaiah 43:21	
Isaiah 48:9	
Jeremiah 13:11	
Jeremiah 33:8–9	
Joel 2:24–26	
Romans 15:9–11	
Ephesians 1:5–6	
Ephesians 1:13–14	

For His Glory	
Psalm 102:13, 15	
Isaiah 43:7	
Isaiah 45:25	
Isaiah 48:10–11	
Isaiah 59:18–19	
Isaiah 66:18–19	

For His Glory (continued)	
Ezekiel 39:21	
Luke 17:17–18	
Luke 24:26	
John 11:4, 40–44	
Ephesians 1:13–14	
Revelation 4:11	

SUMMARY

MAKING CONNECTIONS IDENTITY

People identify themselves in many ways. After reading Section 4.1, you've probably realized the ways you do too. The Bible talks about many of these legitimate differences. However, it is quick to call out fallen direction when people make their differences the main foundation for identity, instead of submitting to God's foundation for identity.

Evaluate the following statements about identity by completing the Making Connections chart. For creational structure, describe how God created these aspects of identity to be. For fallen direction, describe how the quotation bends God's creational structure. For redemptive direction, describe how the thinking from the quotation could be pushed back toward the creational structure.

Read the verses and complete the charts.

Ethnicity	**"[If black people] wish to set their eyes on a higher power and bend their knee to pray to and worship something then perhaps our own African gods are the best way to go. At least we thought of them ourselves, we worship them ourselves, we tell their stories ourselves, they are gods made by us and for us and I think that's the best it's ever going to be."** **—Pauline Aphiaa**
Creational Structure	**Genesis 1:28; 9:1; Acts 17:26–27**
Fallen Direction	This woman believes that ethnicity should determine which god people worship, instead of God's revelation of Himself in the Bible.
Redemptive Direction	**Romans 3:22–23, 29** We can identify with our ethnic heritages, except for the parts within every ethnic culture that encourage us to sin. No matter what ethnic heritage we have, we all should worship the one true God and be reconciled to Him through Christ.

Citizenship (Nationality)	"For humanity in time of peace, for the fatherland [one's own country] in time of war." —Fritz Haber, about his participation in chemical warfare for Germany
Creational Structure	**Genesis 9:6; Romans 13:1–4** God created humans to respect each other individually, with no murdering. He instituted nations and governments to take care of their citizens and interact respectfully, with no unjust wars.
Fallen Direction	
Redemptive Direction	**Acts 5:29; Hebrews 13:17** We must recognize that loyalty to God and His law must be our primary loyalty, above loyalty to our nation. We can work within our government to help it fulfill God's purpose for individual and national interactions.

Sports	"I'd always been the 'soccer girl.' . . . After I tore my ACL, my identity . . . [was] suddenly gone. . . . I struggled to find who I was outside of soccer. Without it, I didn't know . . . how to describe myself." —Rachel Shinnick
Creational Structure	**Colossians 2:8–10; 1 Timothy 4:8** God wants all people to have their identity in Christ first. Exercising one's body through sports has some benefit, but not nearly as much as training in Christlikeness.
Fallen Direction	
Redemptive Direction	**Galatians 2:20; 1 Corinthians 10:31** In Christ, we can engage in sports without letting the identity of being an athlete take over the higher identity of being a Christian and acting for God's glory.

Education	"There just isn't me. Every now and then I want to play soccer, listen to music, or read a book, but when I want to do some of these things in the middle of preparing for the exams, everyone around me says, 'You're a student preparing for [university] exams, you should be studying.' So when I'm prepping for exams, who I am is just lost." —Ho Jae-woo
Creational Structure	**Genesis 1:28; Luke 2:52** God wants humans to learn and grow through education in order to subdue and have dominion, but God never intended them to lose the other aspects of their identities in education.
Fallen Direction	This young man's culture has made education an idol—so much so that students do not even know their own personal identities, which include the skills and traits that God has given them to use in ways besides studying.
Redemptive Direction	**Proverbs 12:1; 1 Corinthians 1:30**

Work	"Perhaps long [work] hours are [a] . . . race for status and income . . . . Or maybe the logic here isn't economic at all. It's emotional—even spiritual. The best-educated and highest-earning Americans, who can have whatever they want, have chosen the office for the same reason that devout Christians attend church on Sundays: It's where they feel most themselves." —Derek Thompson
Creational Structure	**Genesis 2:1–3**
Fallen Direction	The people described by this writer find their identity in their work—so much so that they neglect other important parts of life, including rest, to work more and more.
Redemptive Direction	**Mark 6:31** In Christ, we understand the balance of work and rest. We can work hard without making a job into our identity. We can also rest from work and recognize the importance of using our free time to build relationships and serve others.

BIBLICAL IDENTITY

Read the verses and record what the Bible describes as your identity.

CREATED IN THE IMAGE OF GOD

Genesis 1:27

1. ____________________

Psalm 139:14

2. ____________________

FALLEN IN ADAM

Psalm 1:6

3. ____________________

Romans 5:10

4. ____________________

Ephesians 2:2

5. ____________________

Ephesians 2:3

6. ____________________

REDEEMABLE IN CHRIST

Matthew 5:13

7. ____________________

Matthew 5:14

8. ____________________

John 1:12

9. ____________________

John 15:15

10. ____________________

Romans 8:17

11. ____________________

Romans 8:37

12. ____________________

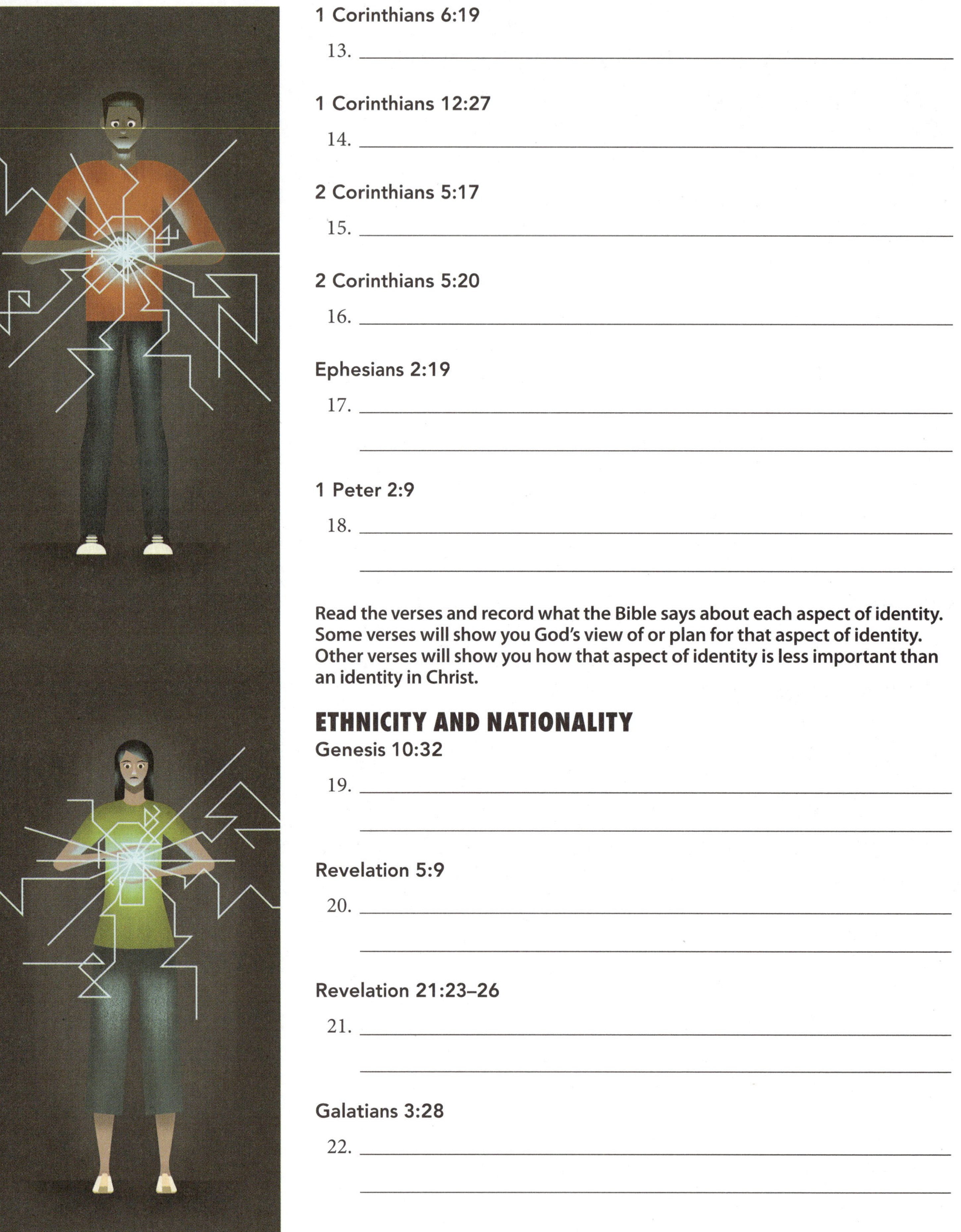

1 Corinthians 6:19

13. ______________________________

1 Corinthians 12:27

14. ______________________________

2 Corinthians 5:17

15. ______________________________

2 Corinthians 5:20

16. ______________________________

Ephesians 2:19

17. ______________________________

____

1 Peter 2:9

18. ______________________________

____

Read the verses and record what the Bible says about each aspect of identity. Some verses will show you God's view of or plan for that aspect of identity. Other verses will show you how that aspect of identity is less important than an identity in Christ.

ETHNICITY AND NATIONALITY

Genesis 10:32

19. ______________________________

____

Revelation 5:9

20. ______________________________

____

Revelation 21:23–26

21. ______________________________

____

Galatians 3:28

22. ______________________________

____

GENDER, MARRIAGE, AND SINGLENESS

Genesis 1:27

23. ______

______

Proverbs 18:22

24. ______

______

1 Corinthians 7:32, 34

25. ______

______

Matthew 22:30

26. ______

______

STRENGTH AND WISDOM

Proverbs 20:29

27. ______

______

Proverbs 4:7

28. ______

______

1 Corinthians 1:27, 29–30

29. ______

______

______

WORK

Genesis 1:28

30. ______

______

Genesis 2:15

31. ______

______

Luke 10:38–42

32. ______________________________

____

BELONGINGS

Ecclesiastes 5:19

33. ______________________________

____

Luke 12:15

34. ______________________________

____

Hebrews 11:24–26

35. ______________________________

____

Write a prayer of thanksgiving to God for who you are. Incorporate the foundation for your identity, as well as aspects of your identity that make you unique.

____

____

____

____

____

____

____

____

CASE STUDY: HUMAN AND ANIMAL VALUE

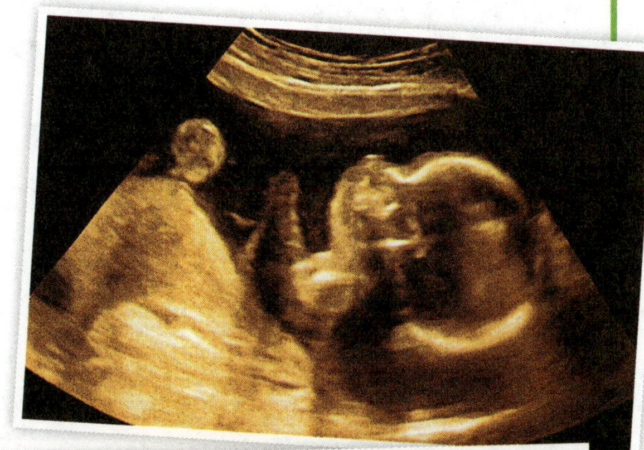

In 2019 the states of New York and Virginia made it legal for a pregnant mother to abort her unborn child as late as the ninth month of pregnancy. The lawmakers said the purpose was to increase women's control over their bodies. They wanted women to be able to choose whether to keep their babies. New York lawmakers claimed that they were simply updating the laws already in place, although pro-life groups disagreed.

About the same time, other people were concerned about the lives of baby sea turtles hatching on beaches. Conservationists in certain areas discouraged locals and tourists from using outside lights at night at their beach houses. Why? Because the newly hatched sea turtles were getting distracted from their instincts to walk toward the sea. The outside lights were confusing the orientation of the sea turtles. Many walked toward those lights—and away from the ocean where they would find food and be protected from predators. Thus baby sea turtles were more likely to die because of house lights on the beach.

Use what you have learned already in this course to answer the questions.

1. What do those who supported and passed the abortion laws believe about the value of an unborn baby?

   ____

   ____

2. What do those who promoted turning off lights along beaches believe about the value of baby sea turtles?

   ____

   ____

3. Why should believers who have a biblical worldview be concerned about saving the lives of unborn human babies?

   ____

   ____

   ____

   ____

   ____

   ____

4. Why should believers who have a biblical worldview and know the Creation Mandate be concerned about saving the lives of baby sea turtles?

____

____

____

____

____

____

5. Why do human babies have more worth than baby sea turtles?

____

____

6. What should change in the situations described in the case study, based on a biblical view of human value?

____

____

MY FALLEN NATURE

By now, you know quite a few things about your fallen nature from God's description of it in Scripture. It's not always easy to be honest about yourself and this fallen nature. Recognizing your fallen nature shows you your need for redemption and can help you focus on certain areas that require growth.

Below are descriptions of different levels of fallenness. Some areas of your life may evidence more fallen direction and other areas more of Christ's redemptive work. These levels will be different for everyone. You probably struggle more in certain areas than in others. Be honest with yourself and with God as you complete the self-assessment.

Mark the sentence that best describes you.

1. How are you participating in your relationship with God?
   - ○ I am mostly consistent with daily Bible reading and prayer.
   - ○ I want to do these daily, but I am not consistent at all.
   - ○ I don't read my Bible daily or pray daily, and I don't really want to.
2. How is your relationship with your parents?
   - ○ Although we disagree sometimes, I mostly obey and honor my parents.
   - ○ I struggle to show respect to my parents and obey them.
   - ○ I don't respect or obey my parents.
3. How is your relationship with your siblings?
   - ○ Although we disagree sometimes, I mostly get along with my siblings.
   - ○ I struggle to be kind to my siblings and avoid arguments.
   - ○ I don't want to be with my siblings at all.
4. How are your relationships with authorities?
   - ○ I respect and obey authority almost all the time.
   - ○ I struggle to respect and obey authorities.
   - ○ I don't respect or obey authorities.
5. How are your relationships with friends?
   - ○ Although I could be a better friend, I have many friends that I get along well with.
   - ○ I have friends, but we don't always get along.
   - ○ I don't have friends, or I don't get along with the ones I have.

6. How do you use your free time?
   - ○ I use most of my free time in a variety of God-honoring activities.
   - ○ I struggle with doing things I shouldn't in my free time.
   - ○ I do things my parents wouldn't approve of during my free time.
7. How do you use technology (gaming, communication)?
   - ○ I try not to let technology take my time with others or the time I need for other responsibilities.
   - ○ I struggle with technology taking more of my time than it should.
   - ○ I spend so much of my time focusing on technology that I don't interact well with others around me.
8. How do you use language?
   - ○ I usually use appropriate language and am honest with what I say.
   - ○ I struggle with bad language or with lying.
   - ○ I use bad language and lie.
9. How do you use your money?
   - ○ I usually use my money appropriately.
   - ○ I struggle with saving money for more important things.
   - ○ I use my money on things that don't last.
10. What is your attitude toward conflict?
    - ○ I try to have peace with others.
    - ○ I struggle to stay out of fights.
    - ○ I thrive on conflict and like to start fights.
11. What is your attitude toward possessions?
    - ○ I am usually careful about things I choose to pursue, and I work at being content with what I have.
    - ○ I struggle with wanting the latest gear or gadget.
    - ○ I have to have the newest thing!

THE RESTORED IMAGE OF GOD

You evaluated the fallenness in yourself in a number of areas. Now, we're looking at the good news. God works in believers to restore His image in them. The Bible often talks about sanctification with the words *holy* and *holiness*, since the point of sanctification is for you to be holy, as God is holy. Sanctification happens immediately when you trust Christ as your Savior—God sees you as holy and set apart for Himself in Christ. Sanctification also happens throughout your life, as you take on the resemblance of God's family in your values, beliefs, and actions. God is active in this process, and believers should be active as well.

Read the verses and record the actions of God and believers in accomplishing sanctification. At the end, summarize how the actions restore the believer to the image of God. If you are a Christian, you may choose to summarize how God is sanctifying you and how you are supposed to take part in the sanctification process.

GOD'S PART

John 17:15–17

1. ______________________________

____

Romans 6:22

2. ______________________________

____

Romans 8:29

3. ______________________________

____

2 Corinthians 5:17

4. ______________________________

____

Ephesians 2:10

5. ______________________________

____

THE BELIEVER'S PART

Matthew 5:48

6. ______________________________

____

Romans 12:1–2

7. ______________________________

____

____

Ephesians 2:10

8. ______________________________

____

Ephesians 4:20–24

9. ______________________________

____

____

Colossians 3:9–10

10. ______________________________

____

____

1 Peter 1:15–16

11. ______________________________

____

SUMMARY

____

____

____

____

____

____

____

THE FLESH

You learned in Section 4.6 that the flesh is always present within everyone—including believers. Believers have a constant battle within themselves between their new nature in Christ and their flesh.

Read the verses and answer the questions. At the end, summarize a biblical description of the flesh.

Romans 7:18–19

1. How did Paul know that nothing good dwelt in his flesh?

2. What truth do you learn about mature Christians by hearing Paul admit his struggle with the flesh?

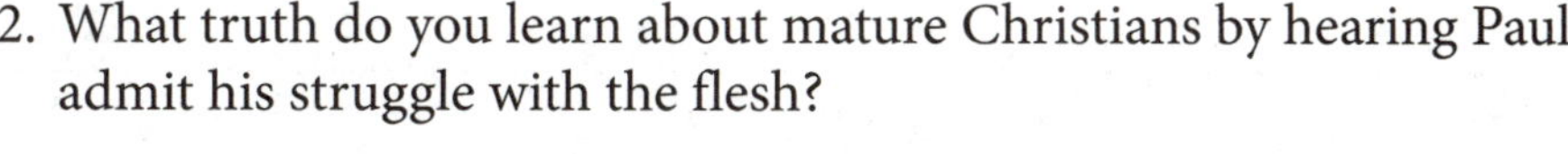

3. How does Paul's wording about what was in him relate to Section 4.6?

Romans 8:13

4. What is the danger of the flesh?

5. What is the remedy for this danger?

6. How serious is the struggle with the flesh?

Romans 13:14

7. What are believers *not* supposed to do for the flesh?

8. Based on this verse, what do you think the flesh will do if the believer doesn't obey the command?

9. How might thinking of your flesh as your enemy help you obey this command?

10. What should believers do to help themselves think and act rightly?

Galatians 5:16–17

11. How are believers able to resist the flesh?

12. What is the battle within the hearts of those who have the Spirit?

13. How does this battle affect believers?

SUMMARY

INNER OPPOSITION STRATEGIES

Read the verses and record the strategy each one gives for fighting the flesh.

Luke 9:23

1. ______________________________

____

John 8:31–32

2. ______________________________

____

Romans 6:6, 9, 11–13

3. ______________________________

____

Romans 8:31

4. ______________________________

____

Romans 12:21

5. ______________________________

Romans 13:14

6. ______________________________

____

1 Corinthians 10:12–13

7. ______________________________

____

2 Corinthians 6:14, 16

8. ______________________________

____

Galatians 5:16

9. ______________________________

Galatians 6:7–8

10. ______________________________

____

Colossians 3:1–2

11. ____

____

1 Timothy 1:18–19

12. ____

____

2 Timothy 2:22

13. ____

____

Hebrews 4:15–16

14. ____

____

Hebrews 12:1–2

15. ____

____

____

Use ideas from the verses to develop a personal strategy for battling your flesh.

____

____

____

____

____

____

MAKING CONNECTIONS APPEALS TO THE FLESH

The fallen world appeals to the fallen nature in each of us. You have looked at Making Connections charts before to evaluate categories for their creational structure, fallen direction, and redemptive direction. Here you will look at the fallen direction in various appeals of the world, determine the creational structure they are bending, and decide how to best counteract them with biblical worldview thinking.

Read the verses and complete the chart to evaluate the world's appeals to you through your eye gate.

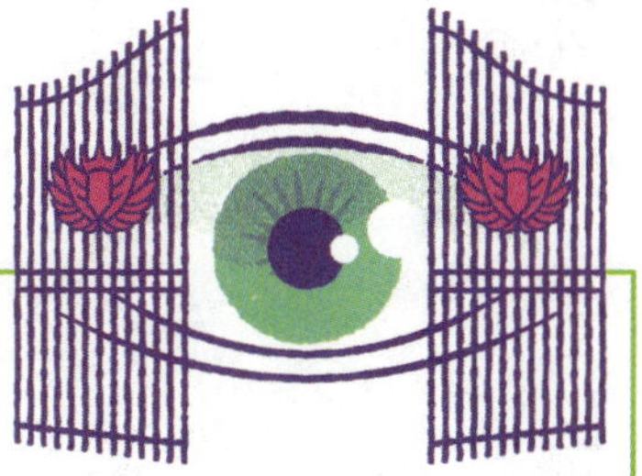

Approval	**The world advertises products to boost your self-image and others' view of how "cool" you are.**
Creational Structure	**Genesis 1:27–28; Proverbs 16:18** Every person is a creation of God and is under His authority. He is to receive all glory.
Fallen Direction	
Redemptive Direction	I should seek approval from God. My view of myself and others' views of me are less important than what God thinks of me.
Family	**The world offers movies and TV shows that present parents as the enemy of children.**
Creational Structure	**Exodus 20:12**
Fallen Direction	This appeals to the rebellion in my heart as a child, which looks for reasons to disobey or disrespect my parents.
Redemptive Direction	I should recognize the sinful presentation of family roles and reject that way of thinking before it affects my own behavior.
Attention	**The world offers popular clothing styles that are immodest.**
Creational Structure	**1 Corinthians 6:19–20; 1 Thessalonians 4:4–6** God has given people bodies to honor and glorify Him. Believers are the temple of the Holy Spirit. They are set apart to be holy.
Fallen Direction	This appeals to my desires to draw attention to myself and to take the focus off God as the one who should receive the glory from my body.
Redemptive Direction	

Read the verses and complete the chart to evaluate the world's appeals to you through your ear gate.

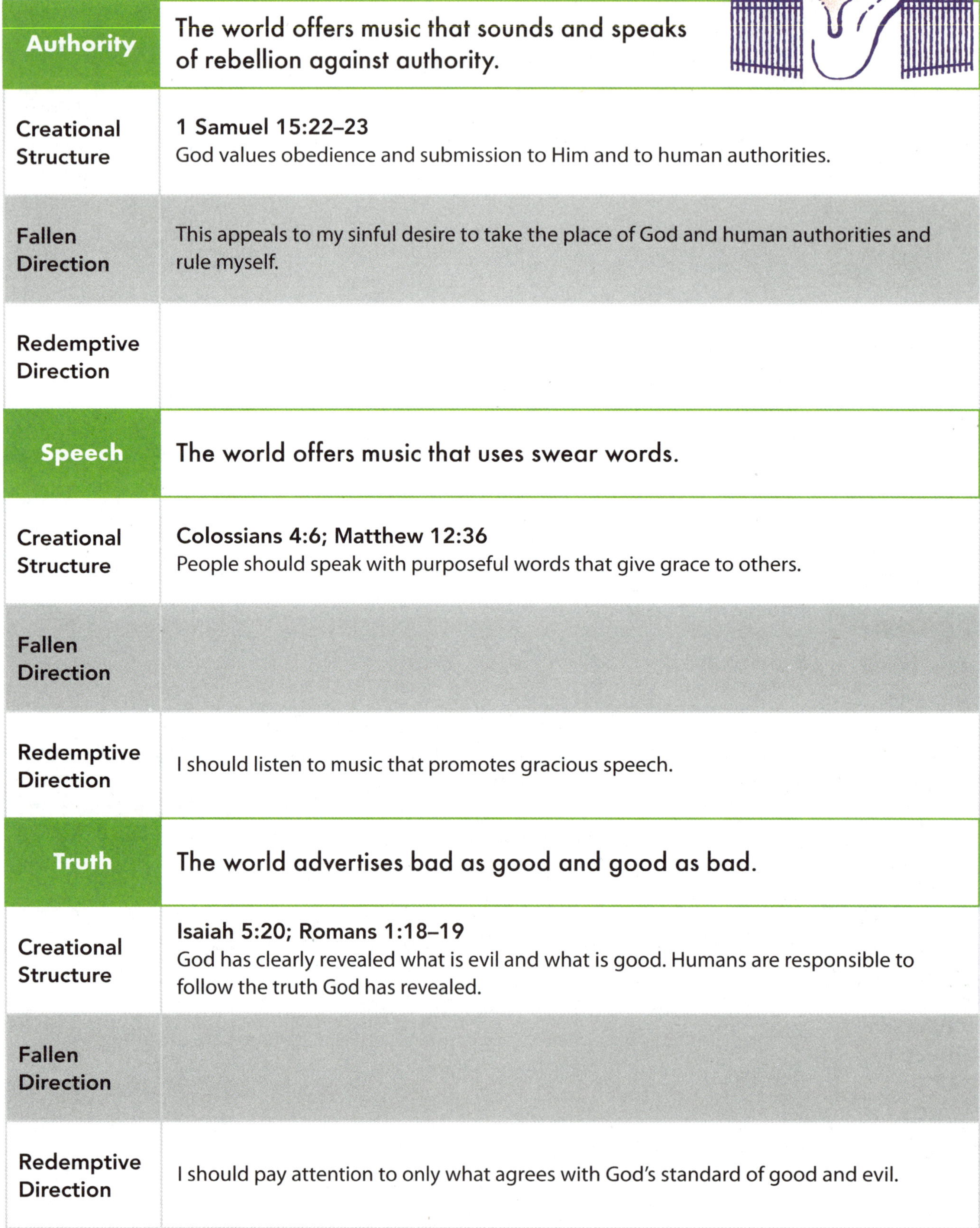

Authority	The world offers music that sounds and speaks of rebellion against authority.
Creational Structure	**1 Samuel 15:22–23** God values obedience and submission to Him and to human authorities.
Fallen Direction	This appeals to my sinful desire to take the place of God and human authorities and rule myself.
Redemptive Direction	
Speech	**The world offers music that uses swear words.**
Creational Structure	**Colossians 4:6; Matthew 12:36** People should speak with purposeful words that give grace to others.
Fallen Direction	
Redemptive Direction	I should listen to music that promotes gracious speech.
Truth	**The world advertises bad as good and good as bad.**
Creational Structure	**Isaiah 5:20; Romans 1:18–19** God has clearly revealed what is evil and what is good. Humans are responsible to follow the truth God has revealed.
Fallen Direction	
Redemptive Direction	I should pay attention to only what agrees with God's standard of good and evil.

Read the verses and complete the chart to evaluate the world's appeals to you through your pride.

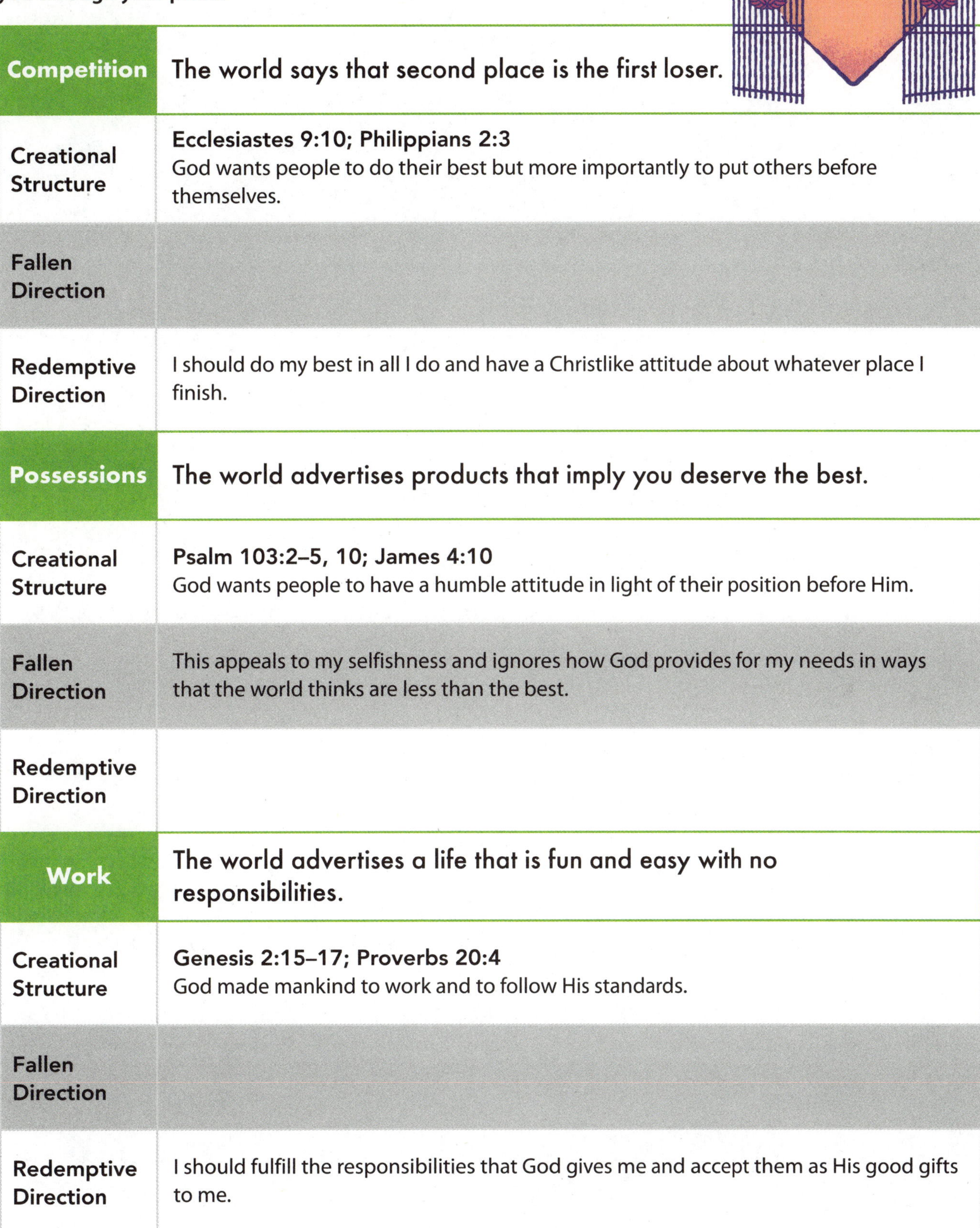

Competition	The world says that second place is the first loser.
Creational Structure	**Ecclesiastes 9:10; Philippians 2:3** God wants people to do their best but more importantly to put others before themselves.
Fallen Direction	
Redemptive Direction	I should do my best in all I do and have a Christlike attitude about whatever place I finish.
Possessions	**The world advertises products that imply you deserve the best.**
Creational Structure	**Psalm 103:2–5, 10; James 4:10** God wants people to have a humble attitude in light of their position before Him.
Fallen Direction	This appeals to my selfishness and ignores how God provides for my needs in ways that the world thinks are less than the best.
Redemptive Direction	
Work	**The world advertises a life that is fun and easy with no responsibilities.**
Creational Structure	**Genesis 2:15–17; Proverbs 20:4** God made mankind to work and to follow His standards.
Fallen Direction	
Redemptive Direction	I should fulfill the responsibilities that God gives me and accept them as His good gifts to me.

OUTER OPPOSITION STRATEGIES

Jerry Bridges uses the illustration of an airplane to explain how a believer grows in sanctification. Just as an airplane needs both wings, so a believer needs both dependence on God and self-discipline to say no to temptation and yes to holy living. He says that throughout the Bible the writers make it clear: "'Man's part is to trust and work. God's part is to enable the man or woman to do the work.' . . . God's work does not make our effort unnecessary, but rather makes it effective." As you battle outside opposition, you will need to work hard using many strategies. But you will also need strategies for depending on God, and the best way to depend on God is through prayer.

Match the reference with its strategy or strategies. Then match each strategy with the category it is part of.

1. **Psalm 119:9**
2. **Psalm 119:11**
3. **Psalm 119:105**
4. **Psalm 119:115**
5. **Psalm 119:133**
6. **Nehemiah 4:8–9**
7. **Matthew 26:41**
8. **Romans 12:1**
9. **Romans 12:2**

A. Depending on God

B. Doing my part

____ I can pray for God's protection from enemies of His work. ____

____ I can use the Word of God as a light to guide me. ____

____ I can renew my mind in order to be transformed. ____

____ I can obey the Word of God. ____

____ I can engage in guarding against enemies of God's work. ____

____ I can ask God to guide my actions with His Word so that no iniquity would rule me. ____

____ I can present my body as a sacrifice to God. ____

____ I can memorize the Word of God. ____

____ I can pray to be kept from temptation. ____

____ I can refuse to let the world make me like itself. ____

____ I can keep evildoers away from me in order to keep the commandments of God. ____

____ I can watch to escape temptation. ____

10. Philippians 1:9
11. Philippians 1:10
12. Philippians 1:11
13. Colossians 1:9
14. Colossians 1:10
15. Colossians 1:11
16. 1 Timothy 4:12
17. 1 Timothy 4:13
18. 2 Peter 1:5–7

____ I can pay close attention to Bible reading, preaching, and teaching. ____

____ I can pray for my love to grow in knowledge and discernment. ____

____ I can pray that I will be filled with knowing God's will in wisdom and spiritual understanding. ____

____ I can refuse to let others convince me I'm too young to live right. ____

____ I can pray that I will walk worthy of the Lord. ____

____ I can diligently add to my faith virtue, knowledge, self-control, patience, godliness, brotherly kindness, and love. ____

____ I can pray that I will be filled with the fruits of righteousness by Jesus Christ. ____

____ I can pray that I will be fruitful in every good work. ____

____ I can be an example to others in my speech, my lifestyle, my love, my faith, and my purity. ____

____ I can pray that I will approve excellent things. ____

____ I can pray that God will strengthen me to be patient and joyful. ____

A. Depending on God

B. Doing my part

THE CREATION MANDATE AND CULTURAL DEVELOPMENT

Culture developed in obedience to the Creation Mandate. It meets the basic needs humans have when trying to fill and subdue the earth. Modern cultures came through many changes over time. But all cultures developed from those basic needs. Many factors influence how cultural products develop. Think about the varieties of local materials, geography, weather, society structures, and cultural ideas about beauty. Each culture is unique because of the unique set of factors of its place and people. That set of factors affected the way the local people developed each cultural product.

You will research a cultural category to explain how humans have worked to meet a need within their culture and, as a result, created products. You should include how the factors around the culture affected the early development of the products. Then you will connect the development with modern culture. Last, you should determine how the development obeys God's Creation Mandate.

Read through the following analysis as an example.

CULTURAL CATEGORY

transportation of cargo

NEED MET

People needed to move goods from one place to another as they made goods in many distant locations.

CULTURAL PRODUCT THAT DEVELOPED TO MEET THE NEED

One main factor affecting cargo transportation in America has been the size of the country. (American states are similar in size to European countries.) Although Americans are spread out geographically, they work together as one large society. In order for Americans to get goods to other Americans, they had to develop road and rail systems. They also made vehicles to move as many goods as possible over long distances.

The Conestoga wagon is an example of early vehicle development. Obviously it had limitations. Trains were eventually built and improved. They could transport much larger loads of goods faster over long distances. Tractor-trailers also began to carry loads over the extensive road system. The interstates have been especially helpful for this development. Later, airplanes were included as a way to transport cargo.

CREATION MANDATE'S COMMANDS OBEYED

With transporting goods anywhere by vehicles, Americans can fill the earth. They can get the goods they need to subdue and have dominion. Receiving food and other items essential to life helps them be fruitful and multiply as a people. To make transportation possible, Americans also subdue those parts of creation that make it difficult to move large loads across large spaces.

Trace a cultural category from its original need through the factors that shaped a particular cultural product. Then explain how the cultural product obeys one of the Creation Mandate's commands.

CULTURAL CATEGORY

NEED MET

CULTURAL PRODUCT THAT DEVELOPED TO MEET THE NEED

CREATION MANDATE'S COMMAND OBEYED

CULTURE

Weeding out the fallen direction in parts of your culture is just the beginning of your task. You'll need to think hard about how to create things that will push your culture toward God's true, good, and beautiful design for culture. Analyze the description of creational structure and fallen direction in the cultural categories. The Bible gives guidance about how cultures should follow God's purposes for these categories. The Bible also shows how cultures bend God's purposes. Use your biblical worldview to write ways you can push your modern culture in a redemptive direction. You can use culture to honor God and love your neighbor.

Complete the chart.

Music	
Creational Structure	Music was part of prepared temple worship as well as spontaneous celebrations of God's work in the lives of His people. Both professional and amateur musicians were involved in worshiping God. Music is also shown as ministering to troubled hearts to soothe them.
Fallen Direction	Music may be done in an attempt to rebel against God. Music may try to replace the fear of the Lord with godless amusement. Some people may twist God's intentions for music by limiting it to professional musicians or to worship at particular times or places.
Redemptive Direction	

Art	
Creational Structure	In the tabernacle and temple, art included images of things from nature (like palm trees and oxen), symbols of spiritual realities not seen (like the cherubim), and even images not based on reality but imagination (like blue pomegranates). All of these kinds of art were used for worshiping God.
Fallen Direction	Art is fallen when it is used for idolatry. The images that ancient cultures created were for the worship of idols. Many pieces of art are still being created for false gods. Art is also bent when it is crafted to bring selfish pleasure to people or specifically to rebel against God and the truths of the Bible.
Redemptive Direction	

Literature	
Creational Structure	We have clear evidence of the structure of literature because God revealed Himself in the greatest of books, the Bible. He used a large variety of genres to do this. He also set the standard for true, good, and beautiful communication, even when having to describe sinful people and events.
Fallen Direction	Fallen literature communicates the lies of the world and the Devil instead of communicating God's truth. Any genre bent in a fallen direction may glorify sin or lead a reader to idolize someone or something above God.
Redemptive Direction	

Movies	
Creational Structure	God mainly used stories to reveal Himself in His Word. True, good, and beautiful stories reflect God's storytelling. Scripture uses both images and music in storytelling. For example, the Psalms are hymns for worship, and God had prophets use object lessons to tell the story of His message.
Fallen Direction	Similarly to fallen literature, fallen movies may portray sinful actions in an untruthful way or in a way that tempts viewers to act sinfully too. Movies can promote idolatry, tell lies, and glorify ugliness and sin. They can appeal to the viewers' sinful desires of the flesh and eyes and their pride.
Redemptive Direction	

Social Media	
Creational Structure	Since God is a Trinity, communication is part of His nature. He made men and women to relate to Him and to each other. Being created in God's image makes communication both natural and necessary for people. God gave people the ability to create tools to communicate with each other and grow relationships.
Fallen Direction	Human communication is also fallen. Social media can be used in twisted ways: lying, slandering, spreading rumors, bullying, and other sinful practices. It can be used for communicating pictures or videos that are unkind or crude.
Redemptive Direction	

DEFINING BIBLICAL WISDOM

Complete the concept definition map about biblical wisdom. Use the verses in each box.

EXAMPLES
WHAT ARE SOME ILLUSTRATIONS?

Proverbs 10:31

Proverbs 11:12

Proverbs 15:21

1 Corinthians 1:23–24

CHARACTERISTICS
WHAT IS IT LIKE?

Proverbs 9:10

Proverbs 11:2

Proverbs 14:8

Ecclesiastes 2:13

1 Corinthians 1:30

James 3:17

BIBLICAL WISDOM

COMPARISON TERMS
Proverbs 21:30

DEFINITION
WHAT IS IT?

WISDOM AND SCHOOL

Wisdom is crucial for a young person to mature well. Biblical wisdom teaches you the truth about reality and your relationships with God and others. It blesses you with many things important for maturing, and it protects you from the dangers of living outside the truth. It helps you act rightly.

There is someone you must know in order to know the wisdom from God. This knowledge is the first step in learning biblical wisdom.

Read the verses and answer the question.

1 Corinthians 1:23–24; Colossians 2:1–3

1. God's wisdom is in whom?

____

Read the verses and record the positive benefits of wisdom that help a young person mature well. Then record the negative consequences of foolishness that a young person avoids by being wise instead.

Proverbs 4:3–19
(Wisdom is personified as a woman in these verses.)

2. Positive benefits gained

____

____

____

____

____

____

____

3. Negative consequences avoided

____

____

____

____

____

____

____

You've learned by now that God wants you to love your neighbors enough to do good works to benefit them. Biblical wisdom gives you the tools to do just that. And so does the wisdom you learn through your schoolwork.

Unit 5 has also taught you that good works can be accomplished through many fields of work. You will brainstorm how school can help someone do good works in a particular field of work. You may choose a field you are interested in, one your parents are involved in, or one you know a lot about.

Choose a field. Explain how school helps build the wisdom necessary to love one's neighbors through that field.

4. Field of work

____

5. Wisdom through school

____

____

____

____

____

____

____

____

6. Opportunities to love neighbors as a result of this wisdom

____

____

____

____

____

____

____

____

BIBLICAL ATTITUDES TOWARD CULTURAL PRODUCTS

Every cultural category of products has a good creational structure within it. The Fall, however, corrupted everything—including the cultural products that humans make. As you might expect, products can be redeemed too. You need to discern what is the appropriate attitude to have toward each product. Many Christians review cultural products from a biblical worldview to help others, like you, choose what attitude to have.

The following verse and questions will help us judge what is worthy of condemning, critiquing, consuming, or copying.

> Finally, brethren, whatsoever things are true, whatsoever things are honest, whatsoever things are just, whatsoever things are pure, whatsoever things are lovely, whatsoever things are of good report; if there be any virtue, and if there be any praise, think on these things. (Philippians 4:8)

True: Is it true to life? Do natural consequences occur for behavior? Does it reflect the natural and spiritual structure God built into creation?
Honest: Is it worthy of respect?
Just: Are the bad punished and the good rewarded? Do things come back to a just balance?
Pure: Does it avoid showing things that are impure or evil?
Lovely: Does it follow principles of beauty like proportion, harmony, simplicity, and complexity? Does it attract? Does it illustrate well the order of God's creation?
Of good report: Does it have beautiful speech? Is it recognized as valuable? Does it have a good reputation?

In addition to thinking about the positive standards from Philippians 4:8, you must also consider objectionable content. Objectionable content includes bad language, immodesty, violence, and the use of tobacco, alcohol, or illegal drugs. Just as in the Bible, objectionable elements in a story are not necessarily bad if they are being presented as sinful or harmful and warn you from participating. You can evaluate the objectionable content to make sure it does not fall into these three categories.

Unnecessary: Is it without purpose in the story?
Graphic: Does it give more details of bad things than is absolutely necessary for the story?
Bad moral tone: Does it attempt to manipulate right and wrong? Does it imply that good is evil and evil is good?

Below is a chart you can use to rate cultural products. If the final total is a negative number, the product should most likely be condemned. The closer the total is to zero, the more you may need to critique the product with careful discernment. The higher the total, the more you may feel comfortable to consume and copy the product. Your score on a product may differ from someone else's because your evaluation may be more or less critical of certain aspects.

	POSITIVE (YES) SCORE: +1	NEUTRAL (NOT SURE) SCORE: 0	NEGATIVE (NO) SCORE: -1	
True				
Honest				
Just				
Pure				
Lovely				
Of good report				
	POSITIVE (NO) SCORE: +1	**NEUTRAL (NOT SURE) SCORE: 0**	**NEGATIVE (YES) SCORE: -1**	
				Unnecessary
				Graphic
				Bad moral tone
TOTALS		+ 0	-	=

Read the excerpts and information from the movie and book reviews. On a separate sheet of paper, label each movie and book as "condemn," "critique," or "consume and copy." You may use the chart to score each product, but be sure to explain why you chose your response.

1. THE AVENGERS (MOVIE)

> As expected, the action violence is frequent in THE AVENGERS, with nonstop action in the final half hour. However, unlike the violent tone in the new Batman movies, there's always a sense of light and good.
>
> Characters have to humble and sacrifice themselves (including risk their lives).

In addition to the information from the reviewer, this movie includes some immodesty, a crude joke, intense violent action (although without blood), and some bad language scattered throughout.

2. THRONE OF GLASS (BOOK)

> There was a surprising amount of gruesomely described dead bodies.
>
> There were visits from the spirit world and demonic creatures.
>
> Celaena Sardothien [the main character] is an *assassin*.

The reviewer also mentions that the author tries to make sense of the main character's actions by referencing her past as an orphan. The reviewer does not agree, though, that the main character should be excused for having pleasure in killing. Also, the characters often use bad language.

3. STAR WARS: A NEW HOPE (MOVIE)

> STAR WARS [A New Hope] is great science fiction . . . [and] the end has good triumphing over evil. . . . To move the plot along, the idea of the Force . . . works; as a theological statement it is a New Age travesty. . . . Practice caution because of the mysticism that forms its world view.

In addition to the information from the reviewer, there are a few uses of bad language and intense violent action and gory details.

4. SPIDER-MAN: INTO THE SPIDER-VERSE (MOVIE)

> SPIDER-MAN: INTO THE SPIDER-VERSE is a terrific, enjoyable animated adventure with clever, funny writing. The story's energy seldom stalls. The movie has lots of cartoon action violence and some light slapstick violence. Some of the action violence is intense, so caution is advised for children. Otherwise, the movie is family-friendly. SPIDER-MAN: INTO THE SPIDER-VERSE has an uplifting Christian, moral worldview. Its redemptive pro-family themes

extol love, sacrifice, forgiveness, doing the right thing, saving others, and getting a second chance.

In addition to the information from the reviewer, there are crude references and some bad language.

5. EASY A (MOVIE)

EASY A is a cleverly written film with some appealing characters and performances, some funny moments, and even some heart-warming moments. However, there's too much offensive content. In fact, some of it is rather abhorrent. For example, there are more than 50 PG-13 obscenities and profanities and strong lewd content, including innuendos about adult activity with teenagers. EASY A also has some drug references, implied nudity and underage drinking. Even worse, the movie contains politically correct, clichéd, self-righteous mockery of Christians, including Christian clergy. There's absolutely no excuse for such abhorrent content.

6. AVATAR (MOVIE)

AVATAR is a visually stunning, but shallow and abhorrent, adventure pitting evil human capitalists against heroic, spiritually in-tune alien creatures on the planet Pandora. Its story, dialogue, and characters are weak and shallow. Also, its New Age, pagan worldview contains extremely anti-capitalist content with a strong Marxist overtone. It promotes group-think and argues in favor of the destruction of the human race.

In addition to the information from the reviewer, there are instances of graphic immodesty, crude jokes, graphic violence, and bad language throughout.

7. JOHNNY TREMAIN (BOOK)

It's about humility and kindness, loyalty and bravery.

It's set during a war. . . . There's fighting.

Rab and Johnny intentionally get Dove drunk to get information out of him.

Although the story ends on a sad note, you're still left with a feeling of strong patriotism.

The reviewer also mentions that the theme of friendship is strong. Also, there are a few inappropriate words.

8. A CINDERELLA STORY (MOVIE)

> Wonderfully written, . . . the movie starts off at a high level of good humor and moral fundamentals. . . . The movie extols kindness, love, compassion, decency, and all the cardinal Christian virtues in a positive, winsome, attractive way. . . . A CINDERELLA STORY is a must-see movie for all ages.

In addition to the information from the reviewer, there are some instances of immodesty, crude talk, and bad language.

9. LORD OF THE RINGS: THE RETURN OF THE KING (MOVIE)

> RETURN OF THE KING is one of the great movie masterpieces that weaves many biblical principles and allegorical Christian metaphors into a magnificent story, but it is too scary and intense for younger children.
>
> Much of the fear comes from suspense, not actually showing blood and gore, although there is some.

In addition to the information from the reviewer, the movie contains some immodesty, intense frightening scenes, and one occurrence of bad language.

10. THE PERFECT MAN (MOVIE)

> THE PERFECT MAN is a light comedy with moral lessons on prioritizing family and recognizing self-worth and one's gifts instead of one's dating status. . . . Romance takes second place to values such as family, self-worth and facing one's problems without running away.

In addition to the information from the reviewer, the movie contains flirting, a confession of unfaithfulness in a relationship, and one obviously immoral character.

11. CITY OF BONES (BOOK)

> There is quite a bit of violence and some scary elements.
>
> The Lord's name is taken in vain . . . at least 10 times, along with other profanities.
>
> Madame Dorothea is rumored to be a witch.
>
> God doesn't appear to have any role at all.
>
> I can't discount the evil. I can't shake off the uncomfortable feeling that the book gives me.
>
> This story had so many other dark elements and references. If it had just been about killing demons, . . . this might've been more acceptable. But it runs so much deeper than that here.

MAKING CONNECTIONS "BE A MAN"

God made men and gave them a specific role. But since the Fall, many unbiblical ideas have developed about what men are or should be. Some husbands do not love their wives as the partners in life that God designed them to be. Some men let women rule over them, even though God created men to selflessly lead the family and church in serving Him.

The Bible shows that God created men and women to be the best team for obeying His Creation Mandate. A husband is to be the leader in that team and treat his wife as God's gift to him. While some men are gifted for singleness, God planned for most men to be married.

In this Making Connections chart, you will evaluate quotations and commercials for the fallen direction in the role of men. You will also determine the creational structure they are bending and decide how the fallen direction can be counteracted with redemptive direction.

Read the verses, which show how men should relate to women, and complete the chart.

Authority	"Love is what . . . makes the civilized man permit a woman to drag him around by the nose." —Helen Rowland
Creational Structure	**Genesis 2:18** God gave the man a wife as a helper in the work God gave him to do.
Fallen Direction	Men who fail to take leadership in their homes have twisted God's plan.
Redemptive Direction	**1 Corinthians 11:3**
Love	"Before marriage, a man declares that he would lay down his life to serve you; after marriage, he won't even lay down his newspaper to talk to you." —Helen Rowland
Creational Structure	**Genesis 2:23** God made the woman from a part of the man to show how close their relationship ought to be.
Fallen Direction	
Redemptive Direction	**Ephesians 5:25, 28** Husbands are to love their wives as Christ loved the church. They should always treat their wives as they would treat themselves.

Leadership	**"At first, every man seems to fancy that it takes nothing but brute force and determination to run an automobile or a wife."** **—Helen Rowland**
Creational Structure	**Genesis 1:27–28**
Fallen Direction	Husbands who do not honor their wives or try to understand them as those they are supposed to lead are not following God's plan for accomplishing the Creation Mandate.
Redemptive Direction	**1 Peter 3:7** Husbands should treat their wives with honor as the weaker partner. They should seek to understand their wives as they live and work together.
Work	**A commercial shows a man making a mess and a frustrated woman having to clean up after him.**
Creational Structure	**Genesis 2:15, 18** God made the man as the one originally responsible for the work. Men are capable workers and should work with their wives.
Fallen Direction	Commercials that show men as dumb and women as the only capable ones are denying God's plan for men and women to be partners and for men to be the ones accountable.
Redemptive Direction	**1 Timothy 3:1, 4–5, 12**
Dominion	**A commercial shows a husband as too dumb to figure out something on a computer, so his wife does it for him.**
Creational Structure	**Genesis 1:26** God gave mankind His image and the ability to take dominion over all the earth.
Fallen Direction	
Redemptive Direction	**1 Corinthians 16:13** Men should act on whatever God has given them to do, knowing that God has equipped them for obeying His commands.

MAKING CONNECTIONS "BE A WOMAN" ______________________________

God made women and gave them a specific role. He created Eve to be a helper suitable for Adam. This role does not make women less important than men—it makes them partners in obeying the Creation Mandate. As you have learned, God gave the man the ultimate responsibility of leading the family and the church. In those areas, the woman is a partner to him and not an authority over him. God has created men and women to complement each other with the strengths and weaknesses of their different roles.

Today, our fallen society wants women and men to be the same. It wants women to act like men in areas that are typically men's strengths. But God designed for women's strengths to be in areas of life that are typically men's weaknesses. To make women like men lessens the woman's best way of influencing society.

In this Making Connections chart, you will evaluate quotations for the fallen direction in the role of women. You will also determine the creational structure they are bending and decide how the fallen direction can be counteracted with redemptive direction.

Read the verses, which show how women should relate to men, and complete the chart.

Work	"I suppose I could have stayed home and baked cookies and had teas, but what I decided to do was to fulfill my profession." —Hillary Clinton
Creational Structure	**Genesis 1:27–28** God designed women to be a part of the team with men to fill the earth and have dominion over it.
Fallen Direction	Women who mock other women who work for their families in the home are not recognizing this valuable work as part of God's Creation Mandate.
Redemptive Direction	**Titus 2:3–5**
Submission	"I don't think a female running a house is . . . a broken family. It's perceived as one because of the notion that a head is a man." —Toni Morrison
Creational Structure	**Genesis 2:15, 18**

Fallen Direction	Denying the order of authority God created when He created the first family twists God's design. People promote single-parent households as being just as good as God's plan.
Redemptive Direction	**1 Corinthians 11:3; 1 Timothy 2:12–13** Godly women will submit to the authority God has given to men in the family and the church.
Physical Abilities	**"My coach said I ran like a girl. I said if he could run a little faster he could too."** **—Mia Hamm**
Creational Structure	General revelation demonstrates that God created men's bodies stronger than women's.
Fallen Direction	
Redemptive Direction	**1 Peter 3:7** Women should not be offended that men were designed to be stronger and protective. Wives should accept the honor their husbands give them as the weaker vessel.
Family	**"A woman needs a man like a fish needs a bicycle."** **—Irina Dunn**
Creational Structure	**Genesis 2:24** God said that the man and woman were to become one as a new family.
Fallen Direction	Saying that women do not need men goes against the biblical design of men and women marrying to build families together.
Redemptive Direction	**Genesis 1:28**

Read the verses and answer the questions.

Genesis 1:28

1. How did God's blessing-command for Adam and Eve to fill the earth reveal His plan for community?

Proverbs 17:17

2. How are friends helpful to us as part of our community?

Proverbs 27:6, 9–10, 17

3. How would a friend wound in a way that demonstrates faithfulness?

4. How can a friend bring joy to another?

5. In God's plan for community, how might friends be more valuable than relatives?

6. How does a friend make another better?

John 3:26–30

7. According to the example in verse 29, how can friends in a community follow the commandment to love their neighbor?

8. How was John the Baptist a true friend to Jesus?

James 4:4

9. How can we break our friendship with God?

____

Proverbs 17:9

10. How can we ruin our friendships with others?

____

Mark 5:15–19

11. What did Jesus expect the man whom He had freed from demon possession to do for his friends?

____

____

12. If you are saved, what does Jesus expect you to do for your friends?

____

John 15:12–15

13. What is the greatest way a friend can show love for another?

____

14. How did Jesus prove that He was a friend to the disciples? (15:13, 15)

____

____

____

VIEWING INDIVIDUALS AND COMMUNITIES BIBLICALLY

Some people and cultures see the community as more important than the individual. The individual is expected to yield his rights for the good of the community. Other people and cultures see the individual as more important than the community. The individual expects to exercise his rights even at the expense of the community. As you saw in Section 7.1, neither extreme fits well with a biblical worldview.

The Bible gives plenty of information about the creational structure—and the fallen direction—of both individuals and communities. Both are important and necessary, yet both can be twisted by sin. As you interact with the verses below, try to determine how they indicate a balance between individuals and different kinds of communities.

Read the verses and complete the chart with the biblical information about communities and individuals. The verses may imply truths about only one category, so you will need to think carefully how to make application for the other category.

	Kinds of Communities	Individuals
Genesis 1:27; 2:18	God created both man and woman because He knew that it was not good for man to be alone. Every person should be part of a family.	God made each individual in His image, both men and women. Each individual is precious as an image-bearer of God.
Genesis 9:6		
Psalm 86:9; Acts 17:26–27		
Deuteronomy 4:7–10		

	Kinds of Communities	Individuals
Ecclesiastes 4:8–12		
Matthew 12:36–37		
John 9:13–16, 30–34		
Acts 12:5–10		
Romans 10:8–9		
1 Corinthians 11:27–33		
Hebrews 10:24–25		

DEFINING THE CHURCH

Complete the concept definition map about the church. Use the verses in each box.

EXAMPLES
WHAT ARE SOME ILLUSTRATIONS?

2 Corinthians 6:16

Ephesians 5:25–27

1 Peter 2:5, 9

1 Peter 5:1–4

CHARACTERISTICS
WHAT IS IT LIKE?

Matthew 16:18

Acts 2:41

Acts 2:42

Acts 2:44–45

1 Corinthians 12:13

Ephesians 4:15–16

CHURCH

COMPARISON TERM
Acts 19:32–41

DEFINITION
WHAT IS IT?

WORD PICTURES OF THE CHURCH

Christ's church is too marvelous to illustrate in only one way, and no single word picture captures all of its glory in Him. Below are several verses that represent the church in various ways. Think through what new truths God is communicating by giving us these mental images based on things we already know.

Read the verses and answer the questions.

1 Timothy 3:15

1. What are the word pictures used to represent the church?

2. What are some truths they teach?

3. What then are some privileges the church has?

Ephesians 2:21–22

4. What is the word picture used to represent the church?

5. What are some truths it teaches?

6. What then are some privileges the church has?

Colossians 1:18; Ephesians 4:4, 11–12, 15–16

7. What is the word picture used to represent the church?

8. What are some truths it teaches?

9. What then are some privileges the church has?

Ephesians 5:22–32

10. What is the word picture used to represent the church?

11. What are some truths it teaches?

12. What then are some privileges the church has?

WHICH CHURCH?

You learned in Section 7.3 that every believer should become a member of a local church. What should a believer look for in a church? This: A group of people committed to fulfilling the responsibilities—the mission—that they have been given in Scripture. See what the Bible says about these responsibilities and then analyze how a modern church is still fulfilling these responsibilities today.

Read each passage and match it with the corresponding responsibility of the local church. Some references will be used more than once. Then relate the responsibility to how a modern local church might be fulfilling it.

A. Matthew 18:15–17	F. 1 Corinthians 11:23–28	J. 1 Timothy 1:3–4
B. Matthew 28:18–20	G. Galatians 6:1	K. 1 Timothy 2:1–2
C. Acts 1:8	H. Philippians 2:1–2	L. 1 Timothy 4:13
D. Acts 2:42	I. Colossians 3:16	M. 1 Timothy 5:1–2
E. Acts 8:4–5		

	Verses	Fulfillment by Members in a Modern Church
Doctrine		
Fellowship		
The Lord's Supper		
Prayer		
Evangelism		
Discipleship		
Church Discipline		

Interview a church member about how he or she practices the above responsibilities in a local church. Write a summary.

COMMUNITY ORGANIZATIONS

Community organizations meet the needs of individuals in society in ways that a government, other individuals, or even a family cannot. They provide necessary services to the people of the community—making their lives better in multiple areas. As you learned in Section 7.4, community organizations include volunteer fire departments, senior citizen centers, homeless shelters, food distribution centers, and many more.

You will practice discerning not only the ways community organizations serve their neighbors but also whether they are operating from a biblical worldview. You yourself may be able to bring salt and light into a community organization. For example, one place that provides a great way to meet and serve people is the local recreation department. Sports leagues give opportunities to both kids and adults to develop socially and physically. And they often provide the opportunity Christians are looking for to meet their neighbors' spiritual needs.

Research the mission statements of three organizations in your local community. Find organizations from different areas of life such as health, finances, recreation, physical needs, or spiritual needs.

Answer the questions with information from your research.

ORGANIZATION 1

1. What is the organization's name and mission statement?

____

____

____

2. How does the organization meet the needs of the community?

____

____

____

3. How could this mission statement be adjusted to reflect a biblical worldview?

____

____

____

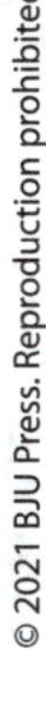

ORGANIZATION 2

4. What is the organization's name and mission statement?

5. How does the organization meet the needs of the community?

6. How could this mission statement be adjusted to reflect a biblical worldview?

ORGANIZATION 3

7. What is the organization's name and mission statement?

8. How does the organization meet the needs of the community?

9. How could this mission statement be adjusted to reflect a biblical worldview?

MAKING CONNECTIONS GOVERNMENT

You learned in Section 7.6 that government is part of God's good design for the world. While it is structural (a necessary result of obeying the Creation Mandate), government involves fallen people, who inevitably push it in a fallen direction. Believers should help push government back in a redemptive direction: to rule properly under God's rule. They can use both political involvement and their witness of Christ. Christ must reconcile individuals to God so that they can rule properly under Him.

Read the verses and complete the chart.

Romans 13:1–7	
Creational Structure	
1 Peter 2:13–14	
Creational Structure	
Deuteronomy 1:12–18	
Creational Structure	
Fallen Direction	
Redemptive Direction	

Psalm 82:1–5	
Fallen Direction	
Redemptive Direction	

Proverbs 29:4	
Fallen Direction	
Redemptive Direction	

Jeremiah 22:2–3	
Fallen Direction	
Redemptive Direction	

BIBLICAL PURPOSES OF GOVERNMENT

Why do people need government? What did God make government for? God gave an example of what good government looks like when He established Israel as a nation governed by His authority. We are able to read about the reasons why He created this government so that we can apply the principles to government today. You will examine these Scriptures to determine God's purposes for government.

Read the verses and explain each biblical purpose or purposes given for government.

1 Kings 10:9

1. Purpose of government

____

____

2. How does this action promote order?

____

____

Psalm 72:1–7, 11–14

3. Purposes of government

____

____

4. How does this action promote justice?

____

____

5. How does this action deal with poverty?

____

____

Genesis 9:6; Numbers 35:30

6. Purpose of government

____

____

7. How does this action promote justice?

____

____

Romans 13:3–4

8. Purpose of government

____

____

9. How does this action promote justice?

____

____

10. How does this action promote safety?

____

____

11. How does this action promote order?

____

____

Leviticus 19:35–36

12. Purpose of government

____

____

13. How does this action promote justice?

____

____

Leviticus 19:9–10

14. Purpose of government

____

____

15. How does this action deal with poverty?

____

____

Deuteronomy 24:10–13

16. Purpose of government

17. How does this action deal with poverty?

18. How does this action promote justice?

Exodus 22:2–3
(Apply the principle for the individual to the government.)

19. Purpose of government

20. How does this action provide for national defense and promote safety?

21. How does this action promote order?

FALSE WORLDVIEWS AND IDOLATRY

Worldviews that are not based on the Bible have basic characteristics that make them idolatrous. They fall into two categories. In Romans 1:18–23, Paul describes a worldview that has completely turned away from God's truth to worship other things. Romans 10:1–4 describes a worldview that is theistic (believing in God) yet still idolatrous. You will analyze these passages for some idolatrous characteristics of false worldviews.

Read the verses and answer the questions. At the end of each group, summarize two things: their worldview and characteristics of idolatry that they portray.

UNBELIEVING GENTILES

Romans 1:18

1. What are two general descriptions of the condition of those Gentiles who hold a worldview of unbelief?

___

2. What do they do with God's truth?

___

Romans 1:19–20

3. How did they get the truth?

___

___

4. What is the result of their having the truth?

___

Romans 1:21

5. How did they treat God, whom they knew?

___

___

6. What was their attitude about what they had been given?

___

7. What happened to their thinking?

___

8. What happened to their hearts?

___

Romans 1:22

9. What did they claim to be?

____

10. What were they really?

____

Romans 1:23

11. What did they do with God's glory?

____

____

SUMMARY

____

SUMMARY

____

UNSAVED ISRAEL

Romans 10:1

12. What did Paul desire for Israel?

Romans 10:2

13. What was wrong with Israel's zeal for God?

Romans 10:3

14. What did Israel not understand, or was ignorant of?

15. What did their lack of understanding give them boldness to attempt?

16. How were they responding to the righteousness of God (which includes God's righteous way to save sinners)?

Romans 10:4

17. Why is Christ the end of the law?

18. How does Christ's life demonstrate the impossibility of sinners establishing their own righteousness?

SUMMARY

SUMMARY

CASE STUDY: SOCIAL MEDIA AND CULTURE

Few things have influenced current cultures more than social media. And few, if any, social media platforms have had a greater impact than Facebook®. With over two billion users, Facebook's community is more populous than any country. Facebook changed how people interact, share, make friends, and develop online identities. It has inspired many other platforms like Instagram®, Snapchat®, and TikTok®.

Mark Zuckerberg is the man behind Facebook. He believes that the next level of community to develop is the global community. His goal is for Facebook to play a major part in that. He believes that the more freedom people have to communicate, the better the world will become. He also believes that the community can come together to develop standards about objectionable content. He says cultures can develop their own standards:

> The guiding principles are that the Community Standards should reflect the cultural norms of our community, that each person should see as little objectionable content as possible, and each person should be able to share what they want.

Zuckerberg's words point to a belief that all people are basically good. The problems in the world come from limiting community and free speech.

Zuckerberg has seen Facebook bring people together who would never have connected before. But it has enabled predators to take advantage of the innocent. It has also made bullying easier than ever. Facebook has brought customized ads to a new level. But it has also divided countries with ads that ignore other viewpoints. It has enabled politicians to engage with thousands of people. But it has also allowed false information to be spread. Refugees of war have been connected with those who can meet their needs. But terrorist groups can also recruit new soldiers to their causes. Facebook has opened up an entirely new culture of connection. As a result, it has been a force for both good and bad around the world.

Answer the questions.

1. What are some of Mark Zuckerberg's basic beliefs, which reveal his worldview?

____

____

____

____

____

____

2. How has Zuckerberg's worldview affected the way he has developed Facebook?

3. Why has Facebook had such a widespread effect on modern cultures?

4. How has Facebook been good for modern cultures?

5. How has Facebook been bad for modern cultures?

ISLAM VERSUS CHRISTIANITY

You've been presented with an introduction to the worldview of Islam. In this activity, you will contrast the worldviews of Islam and Christianity. You may use Section 8.2 as well as additional research.

Complete the charts with answers to the five worldview questions.

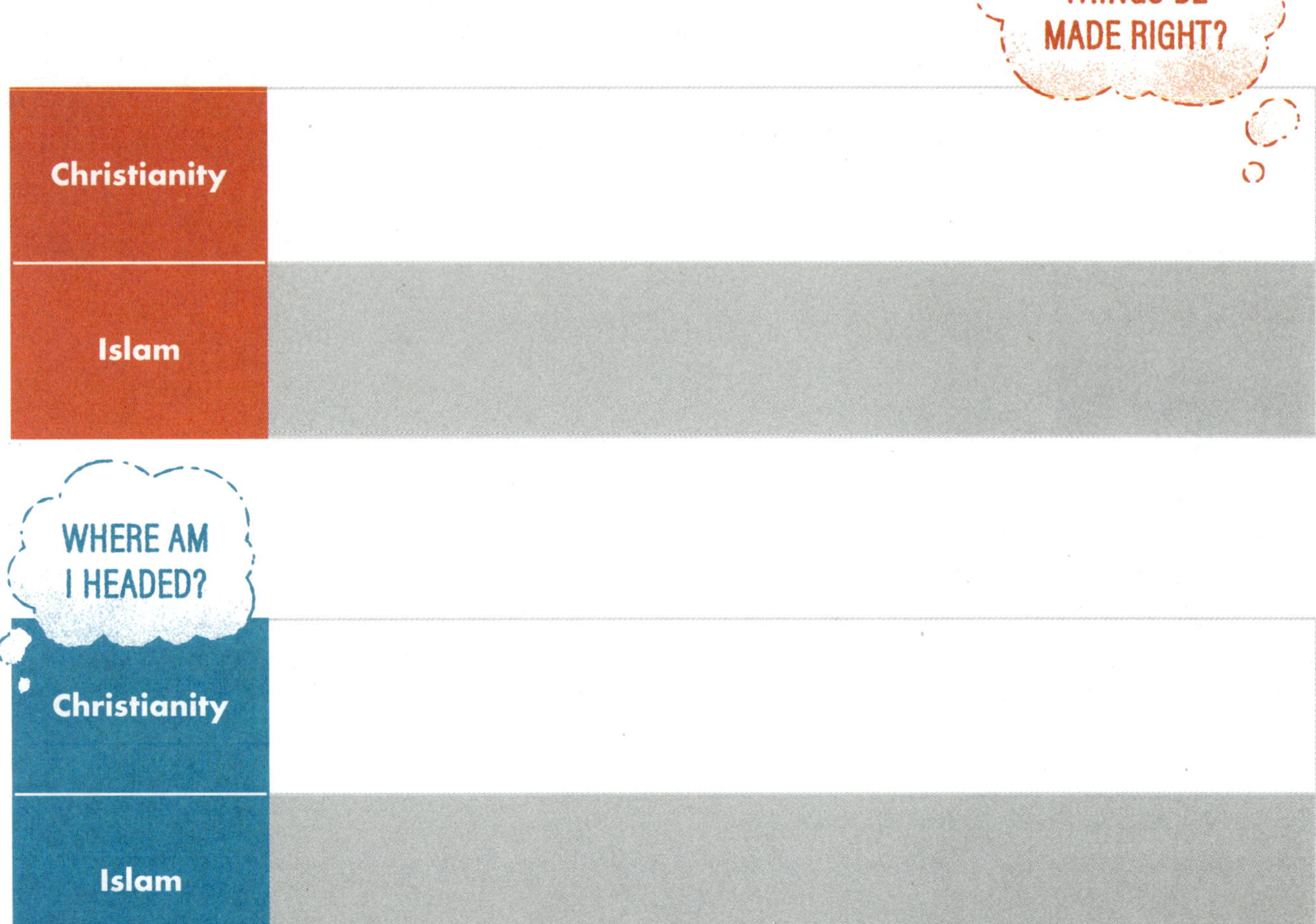

Use the characteristics of idolatry to show how Islam is idolatrous.

1. Denies or ignores God's righteousness (Romans 10:3)
2. Seeks to establish personal righteousness without God (Romans 10:3)
3. Does not submit to the righteousness of God through Christ (Romans 10:3–4)

____

____

____

____

____

____

BUDDHISM VERSUS CHRISTIANITY

You've been presented with an introduction to the worldview of Buddhism. In this activity, you will contrast the worldviews of Buddhism and Christianity. You may use Section 8.3 as well as additional research.

Complete the charts with answers to the five worldview questions.

Christianity	
Buddhism	

WHERE AM I HEADED?

Christianity	
Buddhism	

Use the characteristics of idolatry to show how Buddhism is idolatrous.

1. Deliberately lives in unrighteousness against God's truth (Romans 1:18)
2. Denies God's power (Romans 1:20)
3. Denies that God is God (Romans 1:20)
4. Worships other things besides God (Romans 1:23)

UNBELIEF AS A RELIGION

The Nones claim unbelief to varying degrees. Some do not believe in God at all. They reject the existence of a supernatural realm and believe only in the existence of matter and energy. These are atheists.

Others believe that a god exists or that a god might exist—but humans cannot really know him. No holy book is completely authoritative. God didn't really reveal himself to us. Those who believe a creator god left us to ourselves are deists. Those who believe that, if there is a god, we cannot know him are agnostics.

Remember that even Nones, who say they have no beliefs, are still worshipers. The characteristics of idolatry presented in Romans 1 are just as true of atheism, deism, and agnosticism today as they were of the false Gentile worldview in Paul's day.

Complete the chart with the ways that both types of unbelief fit the characteristics of idolatry.

Deliberately Lives in Unrighteousness against God's Truth (Romans 1:18)	
Atheism	
Deism and Agnosticism	

Denies God's Power (Romans 1:20)	
Atheism	
Deism and Agnosticism	

Denies That God Is God (Romans 1:20)	
Atheism	
Deism and Agnosticism	

Worships Other Things besides God (Romans 1:23)	
Atheism	
Deism and Agnosticism	

THE NONES' WORLDVIEW

Nones deny God and His revelation in both creation and the Bible. Their worldview is based on the here and now, not on eternity. Their worldview lacks a "higher power" that they would be accountable to or be able to look to for help. As a result of these different lenses, Nones look at life situations very differently from Christians.

Complete the chart with descriptions of the Nones' worldview in these real-life situations and how it contrasts with the biblical worldview.

Moral Crisis	
Nones' Worldview	
Biblical Worldview	
Financial Crisis	
Nones' Worldview	
Biblical Worldview	
Financial Success	
Nones' Worldview	
Biblical Worldview	

Terminal Illness	
Nones' Worldview	
Biblical Worldview	
Death of Family Members or Friends	
Nones' Worldview	
Biblical Worldview	

SOCIETIES' QUESTIONS

The following questions are being asked by societies all over the world. What do you think about these particular social situations? You will learn in Section 8.5 why these questions are being asked.

Answer each question with yes or no and explain your answer.

1. Should an elected official create a law based on the Bible or on the majority opinion of those who elected him?

2. Should students be allowed to carry a Bible into a public school?

3. Should public school officials be allowed to pray publicly before school events?

4. Should a professor at a non-Christian university be allowed to teach creationism as a scientific alternative to the theory of evolution?

5. Should a Christian school be allowed to hire only those who agree with their beliefs about doctrine?

6. Should a courthouse, or any government building, be allowed to have the Ten Commandments posted on their property?

____

____

____

7. Should a Christian be allowed to share his faith with others at his government job?

____

____

____

8. Should a public school teacher be allowed to pray with, read her Bible to, and witness to her class?

____

____

____

9. Should "In God We Trust" be written on all American currency?

____

____

____

10. Should national leaders call for national days of prayer?

____

____

____

THE SECULARIST WORLDVIEW

Secularism claims to be neutral and to be the best worldview for a life of peace and success. Do these claims stand up to a biblical worldview?

Examine these claims of secularism from Section 8.5 and answer the questions about its neutrality and effectiveness as a worldview.

"GOD . . . DOESN'T RULE OVER THE 'SECULAR' WORLD."

1. Is this claim neutral? Explain.

2. What does Deuteronomy 10:14 indicate is the biblical worldview's understanding of the "secular" world?

"YOU [GOD] CAN OFFER ME . . . SOME INSIGHT FOR MY PERSONAL LIFE, BUT THAT'S AS FAR AS YOU CAN GO."

3. Is this claim neutral? Explain.

4. What does Proverbs 3:5–6 indicate is the biblical worldview's understanding of God's domain?

"ONLY 'NEUTRAL,' 'RATIONAL,' 'NON-RELIGIOUS' VIEWPOINTS SHOULD BE ALLOWED IN PUBLIC."

5. Is this claim neutral? Explain.

6. What does 1 John 2:15 indicate is the biblical worldview's understanding of a person's loves?

____

____

____

"WE SHOULD ALL PUT OUR RELIGION ASIDE WHEN WE COME INTO THE PUBLIC SQUARE."

7. Is this claim neutral? Explain.

____

____

8. What does Psalm 119:46 indicate is the biblical worldview's understanding of Christian witness?

____

____

____

"CHRISTIANS [SHOULD] CHECK THEIR FAITH AT THE DOOR TO ALL PUBLIC SPACES."

9. Is this claim neutral? Explain.

____

____

10. What does John 15:5 indicate is the biblical worldview's understanding of the Christian life?

____

____

____

MTD BELIEFS

Moralistic Therapeutic Deism holds certain ideas that may sound right and may even appear to come from the Bible but contradict what the Bible actually says. Use what you learned from Section 8.6 to examine these ideas in light of the Bible.

Answer the questions.

WHERE DID I COME FROM?

1. How would MTD answer this worldview question?

____

____

2. How could you give more detail to the MTD belief with Isaiah 44:24?

____

____

____

WHY AM I HERE?

3. How would MTD answer this worldview question?

____

____

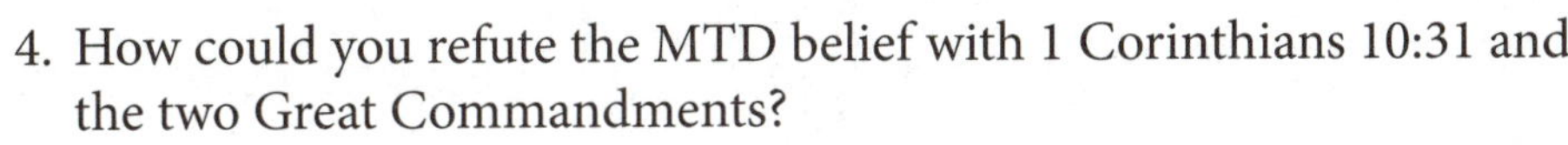

4. How could you refute the MTD belief with 1 Corinthians 10:31 and the two Great Commandments?

____

____

____

WHAT IS WRONG WITH THE WORLD?

5. How would MTD answer this question?

____

____

6. How could you refute the MTD belief with Jeremiah 17:9 and Romans 8:22?

____

____

____

HOW CAN THINGS BE MADE RIGHT?

7. How would MTD answer this question?

____

____

8. How could you refute the MTD belief with Colossians 1:19–22?

____

____

____

WHERE AM I HEADED?

9. How would MTD answer this question?

____

____

10. How could you refute the MTD belief with John 3:16?

____

____

____

NOTES

UNIT 1

Case Study: Fritz Haber's Two-Story View

Dietrich Stoltzenberg quoting Fritz Haber in *Fritz Haber: Chemist, Nobel Laureate, German, Jew* (Philadelphia: Chemical Heritage Foundation, 2004), xxii.

UNIT 3

Discovering Beauty

R. C. Sproul, "Is Beauty in the Eye of the Beholder?," *Recovering the Beauty of the Arts*, lecture 3 (Sanford, FL: Ligonier Ministries, 2003), DVD.

UNIT 4

Making Connections: Identity

Cheyanne Ntangu quoting Pauline Aphiaa in "You Can't Be Black, 'Woke' and Christian," *Artefact Magazine*, January 20, 2017, http://www.artefactmagazine.com/2017/01/20/cant-black-woke-christian/. Bracketed text was written by Cheyanne Ntangu.

Dietrich Stoltzenberg quoting Fritz Haber in *Fritz Haber: Chemist, Nobel Laureate, German, Jew* (Philadelphia: Chemical Heritage Foundation, 2004), xxii.

Rachel Shinnick, "How I Coped with My Career-Ending Injury," Psych Bytes, August 1, 2019, https://www.psychbytes.com/career-ending-injury-affective-cycle-of-injury/.

Journeyman Pictures quoting Ho Jae-woo in "Academic Pressure Pushing S. Korean Students to Suicide," August 10, 2015, https://www.youtube.com/watch?v=TXswlCa7dug&t=20s.

Derek Thompson, "Workism Is Making Americans Miserable," *Atlantic*, February 24, 2019, https://www.theatlantic.com/ideas/archive/2019/02/religion-workism-making-american-miserable/583441/.

Outer Opposition Strategies

Some content taken from page 127 of *The Discipline of Grace* by Jerry Bridges. Copyright © 1994, 2006. Used by permission of NavPress. All rights reserved. Represented by Tyndale House Publishers, a Division of Tyndale House Ministries.

UNIT 5

Making Connections: Culture

Some content drawn from Leland Ryken, "What the Bible Says about the Arts," chap. 2 in *Culture in Christian Perspective: A Door to Understanding and Enjoying the Arts* (Portland, OR: Multnomah, 1986).

Biblical Attitudes toward Cultural Products

MOVIEGUIDE®, review of Marvel's *The Avengers*, https://www.movieguide.org/reviews/star-wars.html.

Harper Collins Alexander, "Throne of Glass—Sarah J. Maas—Book Review," April 4, 2014, https://christianbookreviewsblog.wordpress.com/2014/04/04/throne-of-glass-sarah-j-maas-book-review/.

MOVIEGUIDE, review of *Star Wars*, https://www.movieguide.org/reviews/star-wars.html.

MOVIEGUIDE, review of *Spider-Man: Into the Spider-Verse*, https://www.movieguide.org/reviews/spider-man-into-the-spider-verse.html.

MOVIEGUIDE, review of *Easy A*, https://www.movieguide.org/reviews/easy-a.html.

MOVIEGUIDE, review of *Avatar*, https://www.movieguide.org/reviews/avatar.html.

Harper Collins Alexander, "Johnny Tremain—Esther Forbes—Book Review," October 22, 2013, https://christianbookreviewsblog.wordpress.com/2013/10/22/johnny-tremain-esther-forbes-book-review/.

MOVIEGUIDE, review of *A Cinderella Story*, https://www.movieguide.org/reviews/a-cinderella-story.html.

MOVIEGUIDE, review of *Lord of the Rings: The Return of the King*, https://www.movieguide.org/reviews/the-lord-of-the-rings-the-return-of-the-king.html.

MOVIEGUIDE, review of *The Perfect Man*, https://www.movieguide.org/reviews/the-perfect-man.html.

Harper Collins Alexander, "The Mortal Instruments—The City of Bones—Cassandra Clare—Book Review," August 24, 2013, https://christianbookreviewsblog.wordpress.com/2013/08/24/the-city-of-bones-book-review/.

UNIT 6

Making Connections: "Be a Man"

Helen Rowland, *A Guide to Men: Being Encore Reflections of a Bachelor Girl* (New York: Dodge Publishing, 1922; Project Gutenberg, 2009), https://www.gutenberg.org/files/30630/30630-h/30630-h.htm, 28 [first quotation], 44 [second quotation], 94 [third quotation].

Making Connections: "Be a Woman"

Amy Chozick quoting Hillary Clinton in "Hillary Clinton and the Return of the (Unbaked) Cookies," *New York Times*, November 5, 2016, https://www.nytimes.com/2016/11/06/us/politics/hillary-clinton-cookies.html.

Olivia B. Waxman quoting Toni Morrison in "Toni Morrison Dies: Inspiring Words from the Beloved Author," *Time* online, August 6, 2019, https://time.com/5606750/toni-morrison-inspiring-quotes/.

UNIT 7

Community Organizations

Miracle Hill Ministries Mission Statement, 2019, https://miraclehill.org/who-we-are/.

UNIT 8

Case Study: Social Media and Culture

Mark Zuckerberg, "Building Global Community," Facebook published note, February 16, 2017, https://www.facebook.com/notes/mark-zuckerberg/building-global-community/10154544292806634/.

PHOTO CREDITS

Key: (t) top; (c) center; (b) bottom

COVER

Front drbimages/iStock/Getty Images Plus/Getty Images; **Back** Mix and Match Studio/Shutterstock.com

UNIT 1

1 Elena_Mikhailova/iStock/Getty Images Plus/Getty Images; **2** ollirg/iStock/Getty Images/Getty Images Plus; **9** FLHC 56/Alamy Stock Photo/Patrick Mahoney

UNIT 2

15 (Latin Vulgate) Chronicle/Alamy Stock Photo; **15** (Wycliffe) Public Domain; **15** (Gutenberg) "Gutenberg"/Wikimedia Commons/Public Domain; **15** (Gutenberg manuscript) Age Fotostock/Heinz-Dieter Falkenstein/Media Bakery; **15** (Greek manuscript) Werner Forman/Universal Images Group/Getty Images; **15** (Tyndale) Print Collector /Hulton Fine Art Collection/Getty Images; **16**t DEA / G. DAGLI ORTI/De Agostini/Getty Images; **16**ct © Look and Learn / Bridgeman Images; **16**cb Matthew's Bible/British Library; **16**b "King-James-Version-Bible-first-edition-title -page-1611"/Wikimedia Commons/Public Domain

UNIT 3

53t "The Night Watch - HD"/Wikimedia Commons/Public Domain; **53**c "Tsunami by hokusai 19th century"/Wikimedia Commons/Public Domain; **53**b "John Constable - The Hay Wain (1821)"/Wikimedia Commons/Public Domain; **54**t "Wassily Kandinsky Composition VII"/Wikimedia Commons/Public Domain; **54**c Picasso, Pablo (1881-1973) © ARS, NY Daniel-Henry Kahnweiler, autumn 1910. Oil on canvas, 39 9/16 x 28 9/16 in. (100.4 x 72.4 cm). Gift of Mrs. Gilbert W. Chapman in memory of Charles B. Goodspeed, 1948.561. © 2020 Estate of Pablo Picasso / Artists Rights Society (ARS), New York/The Art Institute of Chicago / Art Resource, NY; **54**b Universal History Archive/Universal Images Group/Getty Images

UNIT 4

71t PEDRE/E+/Getty Images; **71**b Anadolu Agency/ Anadolu/Getty Images

UNIT 5

95 Twinsterphoto/Shutterstock.com